I SHOULD HAVE LEFT AT THE FIRST SIGN

Johanna M. Martin

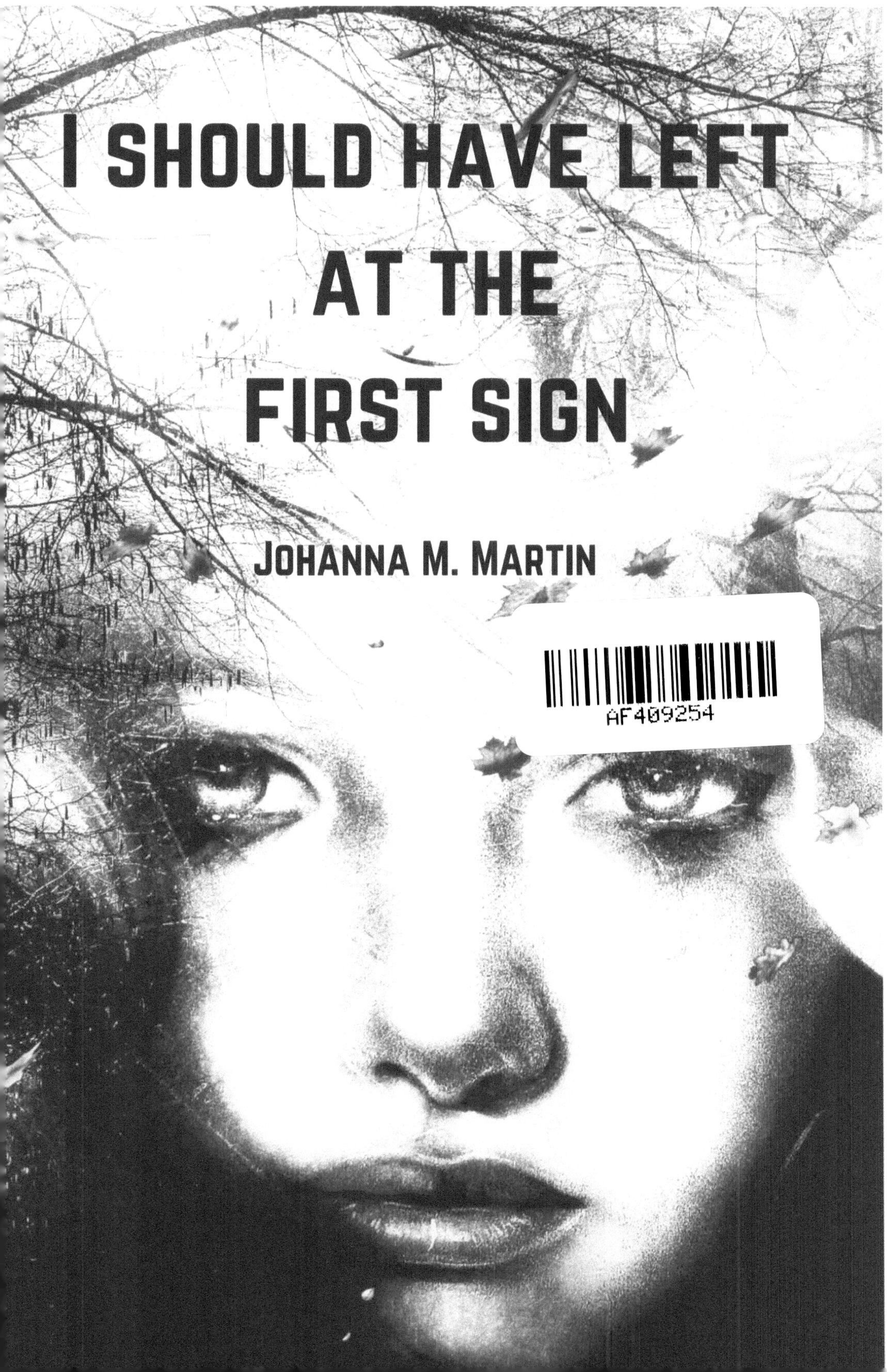

A Thank You
And Acknowledgment To
<u>Canva</u> For The Use Of Their
Elements & Pictures

My Personal Apology To My Children

To My Beautiful Children,

I write this apology with a heavy heart filled with regret and sorrow. There are no words that can fully express the depth of my remorse for the pain and suffering you endured during your childhood. It breaks my heart to know that you were subjected to verbal, emotional, and physical abuse at the hands of your father and that I failed to protect you from harm. I am truly sorry for allowing you to experience such profound hurt and fear.

I know that you deserved better. You deserved a childhood filled with love, safety, and security — things that I failed to provide. Instead, my fear and dependence kept us trapped in a situation that no child should ever have to endure. I convinced myself that staying was the best option, that leaving would only bring more harm upon us. But I see now that I was wrong.

I also want to express my deepest wish that the pain of your childhood does not continue to affect your adult life. You are resilient, strong, and capable of healing from the wounds of the past. I am here to support you in any way that I can, whether that means listening, providing encouragement, or seeking professional help together. I want you to know that I am grateful beyond words for your forgiveness and for allowing me to still be a part of your life as adults. Please know that I love you more than words can ever express.

All my love,

Mom/Mama/Mommy

CONTENTS

ACKNOWLEDGMENTS

A special thank you to my amazing mother. I wish I could have been half the mother that you were to me.
I love you dearly.

Thank you to my brothers & sisters, for helping me in so many ways over those difficult years.

Thank you for giving us a safe place to call home on more than one occasion.

Thank you for selflessly helping me financially when I desperately needed it.

Thank you for trying to talk some sense into me, hoping I would leave that situation, not knowing there were real reasons why I felt we couldn't leave.

Thank you for helping by editing my book. I am very grateful to you.

A special thank you to my family,
for giving us happy memories that we looked forward to every year with Christmas gatherings and camping trips. It helped us by knowing we had these times to look forward to and could freely enjoy ourselves with fun, laughter, & feeling love.

AUTHOR'S NOTES

In this memoir, I recount the painful journey of abuse endured by my children and myself, drawing from my memories as best I can. I've changed the names to protect my family's privacy, as this is my story to tell, not theirs. Through these pages, I offer a glimpse into our struggles and resilience, hoping to shed light on the darkness of our experiences and inspire others on similar paths to do whatever it takes to stand up for themselves and not allow someone else to control their life. I have made so many mistakes and one thing I learned is that you can not go back and fix it. Once the damage is done it is too late to change it.

This book has been written, edited, and formatted to the best of my ability. It is not professionally done like most books but the most important agenda was getting this book done for my children and for myself. I needed to put a voice to the abuse, because it is unfair that this is usually kept quiet and swept under the rug, and even though the names have been changed, my family and his family will eventually know that this book is about him.

Prologue

"If you don't fucking kill him, then I will fucking kill you!..." –   It is difficult to imagine any sane person uttering these words, but my, then, husband, Jake, was not a sane man. In fact, at times it seemed he wasn't a man at all, but something else entirely. These words weren't spoken to another 42 Year old adult, like he was at the time. Rather, Jake screamed these words at our 6-year-old son, whom Jake found out was being bullied at school. My son, Shane, was standing there in shock, his entire body trembling and tears running down his beautiful little face. Jake was seething with anger and towering over Shane, his eyes looked different, dark, not the usual hazel color.

I had never seen him like this before tonight. It was as if something evil was inside him. He has yelled at us before, for many years, but this was something different. He was actually ordering our 6 year old son to murder another child. I could not believe this was happening. I could hear someone yelling at Jake to stop, feeling dazed and in shock, only to realize I was the one yelling, thinking this cannot be real. Is he actually saying this to a child? When your child is being bullied, any typical parent might teach them that this is an unfortunate reality we live in. You might talk to them about different ways to handle this, like, using your words, fighting back, sticking up for yourself.

Jake's solution was far worse. This is the reality which my three children and I lived in for 25 years. Most are bad, and some are so painful I've blocked them out for many years. Some memories I remember daily, but the worst times are the memories I suppressed for so long, my brain will not allow me to remember. I am so worried that I will collapse and lose myself in hysteria. Like I could lose my mind and never recover, cry and never stop crying. In times like these, I remember the suicidal thoughts that I've had so many times throughout my life when reality was too difficult to bear. I know that wouldn't have changed anything, but when you're having those thoughts, you tell yourself it's the right thing to do. You don't realize how it could affect other people; you assume their lives will be better.

There are days I wonder if my kids hate me. I know on the outside they forgive me, but way deep inside they must hold some resentment they'll never tell me about. When they talk about the past, I can hear the change in their voices. It is part of my realization that I am guilty for a big part of what happened during their childhood. I need to express to my children how very sorry I am for everything and, by writing this book, I'm owning up to what took place during their childhood and my part in it. I want them to know that it's okay to share their feelings with me and my part of the blame without worrying they will upset me.

It doesn't matter if it's upsetting to me; they deserve to say everything they may need to, so they can continue to move forward in their lives. I'm wary about writing this. I suppose it could be anxiety, but I know it's so much more; it's the guilt, the fear. I can't help but wonder how my kids will react when they read this. Will I explain it right Will I express what I need them to know? I'm trembling while writing this, afraid of showing everyone what a lousy Mother I was. Will I become an awful person in everyone else's eyes, like I see when I look in the mirror? I suppose It doesn't matter, as this is not about my feelings. I cannot let my own fear stop me from doing this. This is for my children.

They may be disgusted by what I am going to say, because Jake was the man I loved for most of those years. I guess it's true when they say, "love is blind". It is also stupid, sickening, and downright heart wrenching when you love a man who abuses you and your children. It doesn't say much for me, the pathetic person he must have known I was. I am trying to learn how to forgive myself and hoping my kids can forgive me, maybe not for their childhood, but for their mother being too weak, and believing there was nothing I could have done about it.

I believe forgiving someone is not about forgetting what has happened to them, it's forgiving them for their lack of no how and what their actions have cost them in their life. I realize that even if my children do forgive me for my role in their poor childhood, they will never forget what happened during that time. But I'm hoping they will heal a little more from this. I'm going to take you back to the beginning and describe the circumstances that led up to my being with Jake, the hell he would inevitably put our children through, and the paralyzing fear he would instill in me, that kept me from doing what a mother should do... protect her children.

Chapter

1

The Beginning

I first met Jake when I was 19 years old. My sister had decided to move to Florida to join her boyfriend, and I wanted a change of scenery. We have been living in a small town on Long Island, New York, and while I've always loved New York, I wanted to experience something new. We moved to Lake Worth, a smaller community between West Palm Beach and Boca Raton, on the east coast. I spent the first few months enjoying the sandy beaches, beautiful weather, and was working as a Secretary at the Palm Beach Junior College. It wasn't much, but it was new and exciting. It wasn't long before my sister's boyfriend told her he had a friend who wanted to meet me. I was reluctant, because I had never been in a relationship before, but I gave in and agreed to go out with him.

It was early October, and this was my first real date but it should have been my first red flag. Jake picked me up and told me we were going to a house party. I was nervous but I didn't let him know that. We drove around town for a bit, with him complaining that he couldn't find the party, and ended up at the beach. I think this was his plan all along. Now at the beach, he immediately tries to have sex with me. I had never been with anybody before, and told him I wasn't interested. He would persist and I would keep telling him to stop putting his hands all over me, until he finally caught on that he wasn't just going to get lucky. This made him angry.

He started putting me down, saying that just because I was her little sister doesn't mean I have to act like a child. I was insulted and told him to take me home. I didn't understand why it had to be like this. All he wanted was to have sex and didn't care about getting to know me at all. He seemed to only have one thing on his mind, to use me. I was beyond disappointed. About an hour after dropping me off at home, he calls me and apologized for his behavior. He asks for a second chance to take me out. Foolishly, I agreed, and he picked me up again the same night. We went to a bar, played pool and talked. This time around, he was a bit nicer, and we would keep seeing each other.

Jake was my first real boyfriend. He was very excited that I had not been with anyone before him. I was innocent, trusting, and very naive. I also wasn't on birth control. Jake told me he was sterile from an accident he'd had a few years before. He'd been hit by a car while riding his bike. Needless to say, it wasn't long before I found out I was pregnant. Jake was happy, I was in love, and we'd already decided to get married and spend our lives together. We weren't planning on having a baby, but we accepted it without much concern. Looking back now, I believe he wanted me to get pregnant so he could have a hold on me.

Before long, we had moved in with Jake's Mom and youngest sister in Lake Worth. Jake's mother owned an older single-wide trailer. It was very narrow with two bedrooms, one at each end of the trailer, a small kitchen with a small table and chairs, and a living room, not huge, but enough room for a pull-out couch which is where we slept at night, a tv and a few other pieces of furniture. It wasn't the best, but I was in love and just happy to be with Jake. I was okay with staying there knowing it would be temporary. It made me happy just being with him, believing this was the start of a wonderful life.

I was now eight months pregnant, and it wouldn't be long before the baby was born. Jake had signed up for a truck driving school out of state, believing it would be a good way to make money so we could afford our own place before long. The program scheduled him to leave the same week the baby was due, which worried me. I couldn't imagine him not being there with me when it came time to have the baby. Two weeks before my due date, Jake's mother suggested we start taking walks each night because it might help me go into labor sooner. One night we went a little farther than usual and I had trouble making it back home. I could feel some cramping and I knew this would be it. After we returned home, it was only a couple of hours later that I went into full-blown labor. It worked. We were going to have the baby and Jake would be there for it. I was so relieved.

Our daughter, Tara Lee, was born about five hours later. I was elated and thrilled to be the mother of such a beautiful baby girl. I was 21 years old. After coming home from the hospital, Jake had to leave for trucking school a week later. After the training period, the school would connect him with a trucking company, driving a tractor-trailer across the U.S. for a few months at a time. I would continue to live at his mom's place. It wouldn't be easy, but it's what he wanted to do.

Jake's Mom worked the graveyard shift and slept during the day, so once Jake left, I would not have any help with the baby. Tara had very painful colic and cried a lot. When she wasn't crying, she was hungry, and it seemed like she wanted to eat constantly while I was breastfeeding her. I don't remember who cried more, Tara or myself. I loved her so much, but I wanted my mom. I needed my mother. My sister and a cousin who also lived in the area stopped by a couple times and Jake's brother came by once or twice, but I wanted to be home, in New York, with my mother, my family.

Jake's mom never made me feel like a burden, but I took up her entire living room and just felt out of place. I didn't have anyone to talk to about what I was going through or if I was doing this right. No help to figure out why my baby cried all the time. I didn't realize how hard it would be or that his mom could not help me because of her crazy job schedule. I must have cried and expressed my feelings to my mother and Jake because we decided a few weeks later that I would fly to New York and stay with my mom while Jake continued driving his truck across the Country. I felt so happy and relieved knowing that I was going home soon.

***

My mother's house was a cute brick cape with an attached garage on a corner lot, and a nice sized yard. We had woods across the street that gave us privacy, which was rare on Long Island, where the houses are so close to one another. It was not a large house, but a perfect size, in my opinion. My mother said we could live with her, we only needed to pay for the groceries for everyone. My two brothers and two of my sisters were still living there, but that sounded fair to us. We were so relieved that we could stay and, even though there were a lot of us, we never felt cramped. We found it comfortable and homey. It had a nice sized living room and new wall-to-wall burgundy colored carpet throughout the house, upstairs and downstairs. It made the house so nice. The living room had a large couch, coffee table, and a couple of chairs, and because of the nice carpet, if we needed more room, we didn't mind sitting or lying on the floor to watch TV or hang out.

The house had a small galley-type kitchen, with a dining room big enough for a large round table and chairs, so it gave us plenty of room to sit and eat when needed. On the main floor there were two bedrooms, one was my mother's, and the other was shared by my two brothers. An additional bedroom was in the basement that one sister used, and there were two bedrooms upstairs, one was my other sister's, and the other one was where we stayed. It was my old bedroom from when I lived there years before.

It felt strange to be back there, but good at the same time. There were two full bathrooms, thank goodness one upstairs and one downstairs. It was like having our own bathroom because everyone else used the downstairs bathroom. My brothers worked long days, so we saw them in the evening time, and my mother worked full time in the evenings, so I spent time with her during the day. I was so excited to be home. Jake said he would prefer to be home even if it meant getting a different job just so he could be with us. I remember feeling good that he missed us so much, feeling assured that he loved us.

A few weeks later he came home for a visit and never returned to that job. Jake couldn't stand sitting still, it seemed. Even before we met, he worked construction in Maine during the summers and Florida during the winters. It didn't take too long before he found a different job, so that worked out well. The job was in a machine shop, which differed from any work he'd done in the past. He adjusted well to this new job. He was enjoying the work, and learning a new skill set. It was an excellent career choice and there was plenty of work all year round. He received very positive feedback from his employers, they valued his work ethic and his ability to catch on quickly. Everything was going well at this point. When Jake came home from work, he would enjoy a couple of beers to unwind, talk with my brothers as they drank their beer, and it seemed he was okay with living in with my family. I know I enjoyed it.

Tara's colic was much better now. She was so much more content, smiling, and being playful, and everyone enjoyed spending time with her and spoiling her with their attention. She was so beautiful with that blonde hair, her blue eyes and that smile. Even if you had a bad day, just seeing her made you feel better. A few months later, to our surprise, I was pregnant again. We weren't expecting this. I went to see my doctor for birth control, and they did a pregnancy test just in case. As the doctor is handing me the prescription a nurse yells into him and says,

"It's positive!"

I felt the tip of the paper in my hand, as he whipped it away from me, and said

"Check it again."

A minute later I hear those words again,

"It's positive."

I'm in a daze now, becoming overwhelmed. This was the last thing I expected. I was told by someone that when you are breastfeeding, you cannot get pregnant because you don't get your period. I should have asked my doctor, not listened to someone else. In the meantime, Jake was waiting for me in the car, and now I'm nervous, feeling sick to my stomach. How will he react? When I got into the car, I proceeded to tell him the news and we both started crying. We were not prepared for this, especially now, still living with my mother. We wanted to wait until we moved into a place of our own before thinking about having a second child. Well, it was happening whether or not we were ready.

It didn't take long before the fear turned into happiness. We always knew we wanted more children; it was just happening sooner than we planned. It excited us that Tara would now have a sibling. Besides, if you wait until you think the time is right, it may never happen. Soon after, my mother decided to sell her house, so we needed to move out. We had stayed at my mother's house for most of my second pregnancy, but moved into a new apartment before the baby came. It worked out well. I was so excited to have our own place. Now with two children, it felt more like an actual marriage, raising our family on our own.

***

We rented the upstairs of a large split-level home in Bethpage, which included a large backyard. As you came in the front door, you entered up the staircase. To the right was a large living room, which had a large picture window providing plenty of sunlight. It was an open floor plan which led into the dining room. Straight ahead of the stairs was a large eat-in kitchen. Down the hall, there were three bedrooms and one bathroom. We set up our kitchen table and chairs in the dining room and left the kitchen open. It wasn't necessary to have two areas to eat. Our bedroom was right next to Tara's and down the hall my brother, who was also paying rent, had the third bedroom until he married and moved out.

I believed this place would be nice for all of us. It was very spacious with room for everything including all the baby items, like a swing, playpen, and walker. It's amazing how much you need for a little baby. We set up the crib in Tara's room because Jake didn't want the baby in with us. I was disappointed, but at least the room was right next door, close enough that we would be able to hear either of them when they needed us.

***

Before long, it was that time again. I thought I was feeling slight labor pains all day, but I said nothing. I wanted to wait until I knew it was time to go to the hospital. It was a rough pregnancy with Braxton Hicks for at least the last three months, and the pain made it difficult to walk during that time. The doctor said it was because I didn't have enough recovery time between pregnancies.

When we reached the hospital, I gave birth to the baby within 45 minutes. Jake almost missed the delivery because he was doing the paperwork, and they didn't realize I would deliver so fast. It ended up being an easy birth, and it relieved me, believing it would be painful. The doctor said that all those months of Braxton Hicks made the delivery that much quicker. I was very lucky. We had another beautiful baby girl. She was healthy, with dark hair like mine. Tara would have a little sister to play with and grow up with. I couldn't have been more thrilled. Jake had wished for a boy, but seemed thrilled when she was born. If it disappointed him, he didn't show it. We named her Claire Ann.

The joy we had for our new baby girl was soon overshadowed by Jake's inability to tolerate her crying. He started yelling at any sound coming from the baby, telling me to "Shut her up!" I was the only one getting up with Claire at night. I would feed her, tuck her back in bed and if she cried, Jake yelled again. He wouldn't give her a chance to fall asleep. He did not want to hear a sound out of her when he was trying to sleep. I understand that it's hard when you have to go to work the next day, but he had no patience. I soon realized I had no choice but to bring Claire into the living room, every night, the entire night, just to make sure she didn't wake him. It was terrible. How would she get used to sleeping in her crib if I needed to sleep on the couch with her the entire night? Claire didn't have colic like Tara did, she either needed a bottle or a diaper change and maybe needed to cry back to sleep for a few minutes. But that didn't matter to Jake. He couldn't stand hearing her even for a short time. Thankfully, he wasn't around when Tara was having her colic, I can only imagine how that would have been.

It became a routine for me to sleep in the living room with her on my chest laying on the couch. Even on Jake 's days off, I still had to keep Claire quiet. He never got up with her to feed her a bottle or change her diaper. He wasn't a father to her, and she wasn't a daughter to him- she was a nuisance.

I had little understanding of what marriages should be like and thought this was how it was supposed to be. I mean, if Jake had to work and I got to stay home, this was what was expected from a wife, a mother. No one in my family ever talked about how it was to raise their kids. I always remembered my aunts doing everything for the kids and the home while their husbands went to work. In the evenings and on the weekends, their husbands relaxed, read the paper, did some yard work, and watched TV. After dinner, the wife cleaned up the dinner mess, got the kids ready for bed and did whatever else needed to get done around the house. When Jake did the same thing, I thought it must be normal. This was what marriage and parenthood was. It wasn't easy, and I didn't care for it, but what could I do? This was what was expected of me, and I wanted to make my husband happy.

Life was different for my mother; she had to go to work because my father had left her with six young children. We lived with my grandparents, who also had set roles. My grandfather worked and my grandmother made dinner, cleaned the house, and took care of the kids while my mother worked. These days, I see how involved my son and sons-in-law are with their children and with sharing in the responsibilities around the house. I am surprised at how much they differ, and it shows me what a good relationship could be, should be. They understand the partnership that marriage truly is.

I was not working then, but in most of the years to come, I was working full time. Despite that, it was the same way. Jake had little to do with taking care of the kids. He rarely helped to feed or change them even on the days when he was home. Playing with them for a few minutes was one thing, but taking care of them was another, and not his job, as far as he was concerned.

Jake began telling me I wasn't doing "my job" well enough around the house. That is what Jake thought it was, my job, and it needed to be done to his liking. The house was clean, dinner was on the table, the kid's toys were cleaned up, but he always had something negative to say as he came through the door. I don't know why he couldn't come home and enjoy spending time with his girls, his wife, and tell us how his day went, and maybe ask us about ours. Instead, he'd always find something to gripe about.

One day after Jake came home from work, he began complaining, saying,
"I don't think the house is being cleaned
   good enough because I can't smell Pine Sol
   when I come in the door."
That comment stunned me. I told him,

"I always use bleach because it kills the germs,
    I don't use Pine Sol."
Trying to make him understand that just because you can't smell it, it doesn't mean it's not clean. He continued to rant,
  "I want you to use Pine Sol so when I come
    home, I can tell the house is clean."
I couldn't believe what I was hearing. To me it was crazy, but I wanted to make him happy and didn't want to hear him complain about it anymore. From then on, I made sure we bought Pine Sol and used that, but still used bleach too, when I preferred. Either way, whatever product I used to clean the house, it would not still smell hours later when he got home from work. Was I supposed to clean in the afternoons so he could still smell it? It made little sense to me.

I kept cleaning around the kid's schedule of course, and before he got home, I poured Pine Sol in the kitchen and bathroom sink, so he could smell it when he came in the door. In my mind I knew how ridiculous this was, but if it kept him from complaining then that's what I needed to do. I'll never forget the day after he bought the Pine Sol. He walked through the door, took a deep breath, and said, "Ahhh, it smells so good in here, I can tell it's clean." These days, the smell of it still sickens me, remembering back to this time. I continued to use

Pine Sol throughout my marriage, figuring one less complaint, but it didn't stop him from finding many more reasons to get upset.

Once Jake couldn't find more complaints about the house, he began insulting me about my weight and looks. I had lost my baby weight after having Claire, looking even thinner and feeling better than I did before I had Tara. I thought Jake would be pleased. However, he still had insults for me. "Your legs jiggle when you run up the stairs, you better exercise more." He didn't want me to think I looked good. Perhaps this way I wouldn't realize he wasn't good enough for me, which turned out to be so true. Of course, I didn't know that then. I thought if he's telling me this, it must be true. He loves me, doesn't he? He's not trying to hurt me, was he?

Not long after the insults began, we were told that our landlords were raising our rent. Jake would not pay more than he already was, so he decided we would move further away from my family, which benefited him because they would rarely come out our way to visit our new place. We were approximately 30 miles further East, but it felt like we were in a different State. We ended up moving to the town of Medford. It wasn't the safest location, but the rent prices were better, and soon, that's all Jake would care about.

We were renting the upstairs of a large house, with the landlords living downstairs. We noticed an enormous yard, with a fenced-off space they said was for us, so that was going to be nice. When you walked in the front door, on the left was a large living room with a nice large picture window that allowed plenty of sunlight into the room and was connected to a large eat-in kitchen. To the right of the staircase, which led to the landlord's part of the house, was the bathroom, along with two bedrooms. Nothing fancy, but it was to be our home now.

I remember that we were doing well here. Jake looked happier, and I felt he acted less angry when he came home from work. He would still spend very little time with the kids, but was not complaining as much, which made me happy. I was doing my best to be the best wife and mother I could be. Besides taking good care of our kids and the home, I started baking fresh bread every week. It was from scratch, and Jake enjoyed it. He ate it every day for lunch and dinner. I began baking fresh raisin bread and banana bread. I enjoyed doing it because it made him happy and made me believe I was pleasing him. I did everything I could to make it a happy home. Jake drank one or two beers after work, enough to relax him after a hard day's work. I believed I was doing a good job, and that made me happy. This was a relatively peaceful time in our marriage. We had few visitors, which Jake preferred, but nothing ever seemed to last long before having to move again.

After eight months, we decided to get out of the apartment before our lease ended. We were not happy with the landlords. They partied most nights with company over throughout the night and were very loud. This was a regular thing. If we had known, we never would have wasted our time moving here. Tics had infested the yard, and every day I needed to check the girls and myself to remove any tics. You could see them crawling on the grass.

My grandmother had offered us a small apartment that was attached to her house. The rent would be very reasonable. She lived a mile away from where my mother's house used to be, so I was familiar with the area. I took the kids out of town to visit family for a few days in Upstate, NY. I loved it up there, so any chance I had to go upstate was great. Jake decided it was a good time to move out of that apartment and did so during the night, while the landlords weren't paying attention. It delighted me, and I felt surprised that Jake wanted to go back to live near my family. He jumped at the chance to pay less rent. I learned over the years that money was always number one with him. Money always talked.

My grandmother had a lovely home in Massapequa on Parkside Blvd. I don't remember the entire layout, but I remember her kitchen, which was the primary room where we gathered. I can remember the wrought iron kitchen table we sat at with similarly-made chairs to match, with orange flowered printed seats. We sat there with our tea and I just listened to everything she or my aunt, who lived with her, were saying. I just enjoyed spending time with them and seeing anyone else who stopped in for a visit. I would sit there while the girls took their naps. The living room was rarely ever used, but when it was, my grandmother had nice comfortable armchairs in there to sit on. I remember thinking how fancy her drapes were. My place had curtains, but drapes were fancier and of course more expensive. They made the living space look more elegant.

My apartment was beyond the living room, at the end of a short hallway. In comparison to a small Manhattan apartment today, this was a tiny apartment. The smallest one we had lived in so far. It was enough room for us considering it was the least expensive with an open floor plan. The living room, dining room and small galley kitchen were on the left. The living room was barely enough for a couch, side table, and lamp. The dining room had space for a small table with chairs. The bathroom door was on the right. It had a shower stall, no tub, but it was big enough for us. The kitchen had a few cabinets, a sink, and a refrigerator. Down a short hallway were the bedrooms. I can't remember it having two bedrooms, but I don't remember the kids in with us, so there must have been. It wasn't much, but I was happy to be somewhere with my family nearby. If there was one thing Jake hated more than being around my family, it was spending money. He loathed being so close to my family because he didn't want me spending time with anyone but him. If he had his way, we'd be far, far away from anybody. But, for now, he dealt with it because the apartment's rent was the most reasonable we would find on Long Island.

I loved being able to see my grandmother and my family when they came over to see her. Family was very important to me, and I was happy I could see them when possible. I always stayed home when Jake was home, spending my time with him. I made sure our little apartment was always clean, with dinner ready when Jake got home from work. We would have our own family time. I did everything to make sure Jake knew he was my priority, and I spent my time with him when he was home. I visited my grandmother during the day and occasionally would go into her place in the evening if there was some family that I hadn't seen for a while. On rare occasions, I would watch a TV show with my grandmother, my mom and my aunt, which I enjoyed. Jake went to bed early those nights, so it wasn't taking time away from him.

I remember my grandmother and aunt watching this funny comedy show called "The Golden Girls". I enjoyed hearing my family's laughter as they watched this show. I think that is why I enjoyed it so much. To this day, my son and I love that show and still watch the reruns, together, even in his twenties. Hearing him laugh reminds me of the times I spent with my mother when I was his age.

Living so close to my family, Jake couldn't help but let his true colors shine through. He drank more at night and never played with his daughters except for the occasional few short minutes. A few times, my family had invited us out. Jake would act as if he was having a good time, but when we got home, he always let me know how much he hated it and how he didn't want to go out with them again. He accused me of being too friendly to my brothers' friends, saying that I was flirting just because I looked them in the eyes. He said, "If you give someone eye contact, laugh or smile at them, then you're giving them the wrong impression even if you didn't mean to. You shouldn't be friendly with anybody but me". Even though he could laugh, joke, be as friendly as he wanted to be, and that was okay. It was always a double standard with him.

It didn't stop there. He would make sure I thought little about myself. Constantly told me that I wasn't pretty, never looked good enough, and would never be thinner if I ate a snack or had something he thought I shouldn't. Then when he ran out of things to say about my weight, it was my hair he had issues with. Whether it was long or short, curly or straight, he found something wrong with it. With my hair being naturally brunette, he would say how blondes were prettier. If I dyed it blonde, he would go on and on about how sexy brunettes are. It seemed that he would say whatever he could think of that was demeaning, to hurt me and put me down. It was hard to understand why he was doing this. I realize now that he was just a cruel person, who enjoyed making others feel worthless.

One specific time has always stood out in my memory; we were going to a cousin's wedding, and I was wearing a pretty, red-flowered skirt and a white-frills blouse. I worked hard to get back to the same shape I was when we met, and I felt good about my outfit because I looked damn good. Of course, I asked my husband if he thought I looked nice, but as the words were leaving my mouth, his expression made me regret ever asking. He looked at me with disgust on his face

and said, "If I think you deserve a compliment, then I will give you one". My heart just sank, and I felt like the wind was knocked out of me. It made me want to cry.
At that moment, I just closed up emotionally, and later that day when my sister came by and said how nice
I looked, I couldn't help but cringe. When she asked me what was wrong, I told her what Jake had said. I believed him. I thought that he must be right because how could the man who loves you say such a thing unless they're true. Never again did I ask him how I looked, and that day was the last time I ever felt good about my looks.

As I look back now, I realize I was attractive and in the best shape of my life, and I want to kick myself for listening to him. It's hard to understand how someone can make you feel so worthless. I assumed it must be true. One evening, my mother had us all over to her apartment for a holiday dinner. I was in the bedroom with one of my sisters and I caught a view of myself in the full-length mirror. What I saw stunned me. I'm looking at a lovely, thin, pretty woman standing in the mirror with long dark brown hair staring back at me. I can remember turning to my sister and saying,

"Do I look like that?"

"Yes," she replied.

I was in shock, staring at this stranger I didn't recognize in the mirror. Once I walked away from the mirror, she again disappeared and the woman I had become, returned. It was a fleeting realization that I was not the unattractive woman he made me out to be.

I wish I could have held on to that feeling, but in a flash, it disappeared. Now I only have the pictures from that dinner showing me I was not imagining it. Looking at those pictures fills me with regret for being foolish enough to put up with Jake's mean, cutting words. Little did I know it was only going to get worse. I didn't witness any marriages that looked happy as I was growing up, so I assumed this was marriage. Many of my aunts and uncles seemed miserable in their marriages. My grandparents had many issues and my mother spoke little of her marriage, which ended when my father walked out on her when I was a young child. I knew this was not what I wanted. If you love someone- I mean truly love someone, why would you be so hurtful? In my situation, the answer was simple; Jake never loved me. He thought he owned me, like a possession he could control and ridicule. The meaner he was, the more pleasure he got out of it. What kind of fucked up person do you have to be if ridiculing your family gives you pleasure? There was always a grin on Jake's face when he insulted me. He never cared to hide just how much he enjoyed it.

Things began to get worse. He began accusing me of sleeping with his brother, back when I was living at his mother's place in Florida with our new baby. Jake heard that his brother had come to visit his new niece while he was in Texas in trucking school. I had a new baby, who was awake every night with colic, both of us crying often, not being around my family or having any help, and yet he had the nerve now, two years later, to say this to me?

Another time, after we went to visit his sister and her husband in Massachusetts, he made a similar accusation. Years ago, kissing on the lips was a socially acceptable way of saying "hello," so when my brother-in-law greeted us and kissed me on the lips with Jake standing right there, I thought nothing of it. Jake later accused me of sleeping with him too, because the way I kissed him seemed "too familiar," like we had done it before. Nowadays, many people believe it's improper to kiss family or friends on the lips, but growing up in my time, and I presume his, it was not unusual, and it never meant anything. To this day, I still kiss some family members and my best friend on the lips. We were raised this way, and it is no big deal. All this was Jake's warped search for excuses, to make ridiculous accusations.

I deserved better. We started staying home, not going out whenever my cousins or other family members invited us. Jake always had an excuse why we couldn't go, and the fight wasn't worth it to me. He acted so nice in front of everyone, only for him to turn around and make me listen to his newest accusations when we got home. I soon realized this was his goal; for us to not have any friends, not to bother with family, and have no one to socialize with. He always warned me how I better not be telling anyone "our" business.

After months of dealing with constant insults and accusations of flirting and cheating, I began to reach my breaking point. I tried looking good for him, to make him happy to be with me, and instead, all he gave me were insults, accusations, and looks of disgust. So, I realized if I was going to constantly be belittled, I would take control of the one thing I felt he couldn't control; I would get fat. He had told me once to promise him I would never get fat. I knew it would outrage him, and I needed to get back at him in a way he couldn't control. I was so defeated and hurt that I didn't realize what affect it might have on me in the long run. At the moment, I only thought about the immediate reaction... and I wanted to piss him off.

I put my plan into action. One night, with the girls in bed, we were sitting on the couch watching TV. I got up from my seat, went into the kitchen and grabbed a Twinkie. Jake just looked at me and said, "What are you

doing?" He always had desert after dinner, but I wasn't allowed, because he would go into a tirade about how terrible I looked and how I needed to eat better. He believed a woman's diet should be mostly salad and that's it. As I ate the Twinkie, I had goosebumps running through me as his glaring stare and outrage were showing, but I didn't let it deter me. I then went back into the kitchen and grabbed another one. As I opened the package, I saw his face grow bright red with anger until he finally let loose. He turned to me and screamed,
  "Don't you dare eat that!"
For the first time, I felt in control, I was elated. I was doing something that made him angry, and he couldn't stop me. I turned to him and said,
  "What's the point in looking good for you if you're just going to accuse me of cheating or flirting with someone. I'm tired of it, so I might as well eat what-ever I want."
It felt so good to finally take back some control from him.
     Of course, this would backfire on me. I gained weight, and expected him to continue ridiculing my appearance, but the constant accusations of cheating and flirting never stopped. It didn't matter if I looked good or not, as he loved to say, "I was his virgin" and no one else was ever going to have me. Marrying the only

man I ever slept with had meant something special to me until Jake became so obsessed. He needed to make sure it always stayed that way. This obsessive and controlling nature of thinking he owned me. He would accuse me of cheating daily, even though I'm raising two kids with almost no help from him. Today, I know that he did this so he could hear me tell him over and over that he was the only one. The number of times I had to reassure Jake during my marriage that I was "his virgin" wasn't just disturbing, it was downright sickening.

Chapter

2

A Fresh Start

Jake wanted to leave New York, and my family, this wasn't long after I started putting on weight. He had found out that the machine shop he worked in had another shop in Stowe, Vermont. He asked his boss for a transfer, and it was granted. However, we didn't stay in Vermont more than a few months before Jake decided he wanted to move back to his home State of Maine. I was so sick of moving but I hoped that by going back to his hometown, he might be happier. This, as it turns out, wasn't the case.

Once again, it started out okay. He acted happy to be back in Maine and wanted us to live at his father's old camp, where he didn't have to pay rent. That was a big plus in Jake's eyes and, most likely, the main reason we moved to Maine. This camp had been in the family during his childhood and his father had promised to leave it to his kids. Jake didn't believe that would happen. The camp was located a half mile down a one-lane bumpy dirt road. It had lots of ruts and rocks along the way. When you came to the end, you got to his father's place, a dead end with lots of privacy.

It was on a nice quiet lake, right near the water with a small dirt front yard. The camp was a small one-story gray building, and not much to look at. The best feature besides the lake were the nice size windows for sunlight and the view of the lake. From outside, you walked into the living room through the only door that faced the driveway. Inside was an old worn-out couch, two chairs, a coffee table, and a wood stove for heat. To the right you entered the kitchen. It was old, with a small kitchen table and chairs at one end and a sink, a couple of cabinets and an old refrigerator. Two small windows were at each end that barely brought sunlight into the kitchen. There was old linoleum flooring, which was in terrible shape. From the kitchen was a doorway that led into the only bedroom. It was nothing to speak of, just a room with two mattresses on metal bed frames. No dresser for our clothes; just shelving.

Jake's family had never used the camp in winter, and for good reason. It didn't have insulation, running water, or a bathroom. All we had was lake water, which we had to boil for cooking and washing dishes. We had an old outhouse that had been there for many years. To say this was difficult to get used to is an understatement. During the wintertime, we needed to cut a hole in the ice so we could lug in buckets of water to boil. Plastic needed to go on the windows to keep the cold air outside, so you couldn't enjoy any view during that time. The only good thing was the wood stove, which heated the place because it was small. In the bedroom, we slept on one side of the room and the girls on the other side. Jake hung a curtain up by their bed to give us privacy.

During the night we literally used a pot to pee in so we didn't have to use the outhouse during the frigid, dark night. In the spring, Jake built a new outhouse which was a bit better, but was still nothing compared to a working bathroom.

I never complained about living there, not that it would do me any good, anyways. So, I thought of it as an adventure, something we did as a family. We managed pretty well, despite the inconvenience of no indoor plumbing. I still just wanted to make Jake happy and was more than willing to go without certain amenities to do that. My relatives thought I was crazy to live that way, but I never looked at it as a terrible thing. We needed to do this, so we could save for our own beautiful home one day. Sacrifice and hard work were necessary to save for the good things in life. That's how I looked at it. It excited me, the thought of not having to live with anyone else. We lived there for around a year, with Jake working and me, staying home with the girls. Jake worked the second shift at a machine shop, but because of the travel, didn't get home until around 2 a.m. I remember always feeling nervous at night, all alone with the girls.

There was no one else around when the other campers left for the winter. Campers only stayed until late September or early October and wouldn't return until the end of May. You didn't have access to drive in and out of this road during the winter, because of ice, snow, or mud. Jake had to park at the top by the main road and walk down the seasonal road to the camp. To get groceries while Jake went to work, a friend of ours picked us up at the top of the road. I pulled Tara and Claire on the sled the half mile to the top and brought an extra sled to pull the girls and the groceries back down when we got back. That was our routine. It wasn't easy, but we did what we had to do.

I don't remember how we were getting along at that point because Jake worked long hours, and I spent most of my time taking care of the kids and the camp, as usual. I know he liked us secluded from everyone else and rarely having a visitor. He split the land we bought into two lots and built a nice split-level ranch for the first house and was planning on building a ranch with a walk-out basement on the second lot. My favorite house was always a country-style cape with a big front porch. I was eager for us to have our own home one day. If there was one redeeming quality about the man I married, It was that he was an excellent carpenter and could build very nice homes.

The person who bought the split-level home lived in Connecticut and planned on retiring here in Maine. In the meantime, he offered to let us rent it from him until he was ready to move here. It thrilled us to do that, seeing that Jake was building another house on the piece of land next door. It would be very convenient. He gave us a good price on the rent too, so that was helpful.

It was a nice sized house. It had big Anderson windows in it and we stained the shingles on the outside an attractive gray-blue color. I can still remember dipping every single shingle by hand. What a project that was. Taking care of the house and the kids wasn't enough for Jake, he made me work on the houses with him, while trying to monitor the girls as they ran around and played. It was difficult, to say the least. I didn't enjoy working with him because he had no patience and yelled all the time about everything. I am terrified of heights, yet he would make me climb up high ladders, and get so mad if I hesitated, because I feared heights. Of course, I did all the gopher work. Go for this and get me that. It wasn't fun, but I thought of it as working towards us having a home of our own. I didn't know then that Jake had no intention of ever building us our own home.

Jake seemed pleased about building these homes, but that didn't matter. He continued to drink more and more, almost drunk every night, and still spent little time with the girls. They wanted any attention he would give since, to them, any attention was better than none.

There wasn't much verbal abuse towards them at that time; he would more so just ignore them, which to me is emotional abuse. Kids are smart, they know when their dad doesn't want anything to do with them unless it benefits him. He had no desire or interest in spending time with them. He neglected them. Most of the time, the kids were an inconvenience to Jake, and only were welcome when he wanted them to get him something. They could go grab him a beer out of the refrigerator or change the channel for him, things like that. Tara and Claire had witnessed him drunk frequently, but were too young to understand, and they would sometimes think it was funny. I think the most fun they ever had was when he was almost passed out and drunk. One time I can recall him being passed out on the carpet in the living room. He had been playing with them for a few minutes, but was too drunk to continue. I can't remember how old they were, maybe 8 & 9, but they each took one of his arms and were dragging him down the hallway. He was helping them along with it in his stupor. They were laughing and were just so happy because they thought it was all playing, which didn't happen very often. They didn't realize how drunk he was. I should have stopped it, but in that moment, they looked so happy. I can still see them in their white flowered zip-up bathrobes, ready for bed. Tara with her long blonde hair and Claire with her medium-length dark brown hair. They had such big smiles on their faces, laughing to each other over how silly Daddy looked. They were having fun, which didn't happen often. I remember taking a picture of them while they were doing this, I wanted Jake to see it because he wouldn't remember this the next day, like so many other times he would get drunk and not remember. I wanted him to see that this was not the way to have fun with the girls.

***

I had started working evenings as a cashier at a convenience store, leaving the girls home alone with Jake. We needed the money, but I still regret ever leaving them in his care. Not only was Jake constantly drunk at home, but he would also be drinking and driving with my two little girls in the car while I was at work. He would show up at my job to check up on me, and brag that he could drink and drive with them and that there was nothing I could do about it. I was petrified, knowing that he would do this and thought so little of his daughters. I would yell and beg him not to do it, and then I would find out he did it again.

One day while I was at work, I received a phone call from some friends of his, telling me he just showed up at their house so drunk that he couldn't even stand. They said he tried to leave, but they refused to let him. I left work and, when I arrived there, he was still too drunk to walk on his own. How he ever drove there without having an accident was just luck and, most likely, a miracle from God that saved my girls that night. I refused to let things continue like this. He was going to kill my little girls if I kept working at the store. So, I quit.

I was too afraid to stand up to Jake. I believed I had to do whatever he told me to do, and working was something he wanted me to do, but to continue to leave my girls alone with him was out of the question. After he kept drinking and driving with my girls, I stood up to Jake about his drinking. We were at his sister's house in the town of South China. He had way too much to drink. When it was time to leave, I wanted to drive home, but he refused. He started screaming and yelling at me to get in the car, but I held my ground. He got in the car and drove off drunk and angry while I was left standing there with the two girls, shaking in my boots because I had embarrassed him in front of his family and said "No" to him. I was nervous, thinking of what may happen when I got home. I never knew when the screaming and yelling could turn physical. He had raised his hand in front of my face, as if about to hit me, and then restrained himself. To be honest, I can't remember what happened when I got home that night.

I had no choice but to keep working and keep my kids safe. I signed up for a Certified Nurse's Assistant Course which takes about six weeks after which I began working as a "CNA". I worked the graveyard shift in a nursing home in Augusta so I could be home with the kids during the day. Jake continued to drink and drive, but at least not with the kids anymore. He had no reason to bring them with him anymore, because I was home during most of the evening, napping before work. If he went out, he could leave the kids with me. He was always home on time for me to leave for work because he wanted me to make money. Unfortunately, I had to leave the girls with him when I left each night for work regardless of his drinking. I will always feel guilty about having to leave my kids alone with him, but in this town, hundreds of miles away from any of my family that could watch after the kids, I had little choice. During this time in our marriage, I took the brunt of Jake's bad moods, not the girls.

Not long after starting as a CNA, one of my sisters had moved nearby me in Maine. I was so happy to have some of my family close to me. My mother and other siblings would occasionally visit my sister, so I'd get to see them too, but Jake didn't like me spending time with them. One time, he heard a broadcast offering free land being given away to anyone willing to move to British Columbia because they were trying to get people to move there. Jake relished the idea of living a secluded life on some free land. He glorified the notion of having to hunt for our food and survive in the wilderness. When he found out how much I detested the thought, he began threatening me with the idea. He would say if I tried to leave him, he would take the girls to the mountains, build a shack to live in with them, and I would never see them again. Just remembering that now, makes me sick to my stomach.

I believed his threat and knew that I could never leave him. I knew that he'd take the girls, and with no one to protect them, God only knows what would have happened to them. No family, no friends. As far as he was concerned, the girls were only useful for doing chores. They'd have to make his meals, do the laundry, and follow his orders or else. That would be their existence. It was a sickening and frightful threat and of course, he was capable of kidnapping the girls. I knew that I would just have to placate him, deal with his behaviors, always try to smooth things over and bend to his will. I had to keep him in Maine and keep trying to please him. My fear always controlled me. The fear of what was happening, and especially the fear of what could happen.

Of course, Jake was still his miserable self. It upset him that I had gained weight and didn't look good enough for him. He felt I wasn't up to his standards of what a wife should be. We had a terrible fight once because I complained while shoveling our very long, wide driveway that it was hurting my back. Jake was too cheap to pay someone to plow it, so he and I always had to shovel it. This time the snow was the wet slushy snow and very heavy, so I was really struggling. I said to him," My back is killing me. I can't do this." He started screaming at me, threw his glass in the sink and as it shattered, he started telling me how disgusting I was, and that I couldn't shovel the driveway because I was so out of shape. I had shoveled this driveway many times, but a foot of heavy snow was too much for me. Why should I have to work full time, do all the housework, take care of the kids, plus help him with the outside work? I was doing all of my "responsibilities" without his help, and yet he needed my help to shovel in the winter, rake leaves in the fall and stack wood for the wood stoves we have in our homes. It was rare that I ever complained, but this particular day was the last straw.

His screaming and carrying on frightened me and I was unsure of what to do, so I packed the girls up and we went to my sister's house. I asked her, if I were to leave him, what was the chance of us staying with her until I figured things out. She emphatically welcomed us but that was short-lived. Soon after that argument, I found out I was pregnant. Jake wanted a boy, so I agreed, but I wasn't sure about bringing another child into this household. I was nervous and unsure of what I was going to do. How could I have another baby now? I kept thinking about how I needed to call and make an appointment for an abortion.

***

After telling Jake I was pregnant, he was excited at the thought of a boy. He begged me to come home and to be just as excited, because everything would be better and he was sorry for how he was treating me. He said everything he knew I wanted to hear, and I wanted to believe it. I was foolish and always had this way of picturing that it could happen. How he could actually change. He just needed to realize that he had a family who loved him. We could be a happy family if he would just lighten up and see the love surrounding him. I knew deep inside that I could never go through with the abortion, so what choice did I have? So, I returned home. Jake tried to be better for a short time, but it didn't last long. I hate knowing that I loved him so much back then, that I would keep forgiving him over and over, no matter how much he hurt me.

Soon after, we were notified that we'd have to move out of the house we were renting. The homeowner had been diagnosed with terminal cancer and he needed to sell the house as quickly as possible. It was upsetting because he was such a nice man, and we were sad for him. Jake had bought more land in Windsor. This land was more expensive because it was in a private development with underground electricity, which was nice. The land was comprised of two separate lots, and he was planning to build two houses – one to sell, and the other for us to keep. We were finally going to have our own home. It was a perfect location, with deeded rights to a lake. Each lot had five acres of property, so you didn't even see the house next to you, which meant great privacy.

Jake also wanted to buy his father's camp, where we were living before. His father had promised to leave it to Jake and his sisters, but Jake didn't think that would ever happen, so he decided he had to have it. Even though we were in debt with this other land, he bought the camp. I'm not sure how we managed it but the camp was ours. Jake wanted to tear it down and build a new home in its place. He said we would stay there until "our forever home" was built on the other piece of land. At the time, the camp was so infested with carpenter ants that Jake got permission from the town to burn it down, with the stipulation that we move the new place back further away from the water. So, Jake built a new lake house. We moved from the rental to the new lake house in Whitefield and lived there for a few years while Jake completed the two houses in Windsor.

***

The lake house that Jake built was a beautiful chalet-style home with enormous windows that looked out over the lake. It was small, but lovely. He used nice clapboard siding and built a deck on the side of the house facing the driveway where you enter the home. When you walked in the door, you entered a large living room area. The ceiling was vaulted with wood beams that ran from one end to the other. It had an open floor plan and a spiral staircase that led to a loft bedroom upstairs. To the right was a small, very nice kitchen with poplar wood cabinets. It didn't have a traditional oven; instead, there was a stove-top range on the island which faced the living room, and a convection oven hung under the cabinets. Beyond the kitchen was a small hallway that led to the bathroom and a bedroom. The bathroom had a shower stall instead of a tub, along with a stacked washer and dryer. It was perfect for what we needed. On the left was the bedroom, which was large, with one big window and a decent closet. Straight across from the kitchen was the dining room area. A chimney and hearth, with a nice wood stove was on the back wall and had a window on each side. On this wall, Jake put a variety of small wood bricks to make it stand out. I loved it.

Up the spiral staircase was a loft bedroom. You could see the lake through the large, triangular-shaped windows. We started out with the girls having the upstairs bedroom and we had the downstairs one, but after we had the baby, we moved upstairs since there was plenty of room for the crib and had the girls sleep downstairs. I loved this home. To this day, it is the nicest house Jake has ever built, by far.

Like always, there were some drawbacks to moving here. Tara and Claire had to switch schools, which was hard on them. We had thought we could keep them in the Windsor school, which was better, because we owned property there and were building a home. However, we were told that unless we were living there, we could not keep them in that school. They made the most of it, though. They loved the new house, and loved the lake. It was like being on vacation, able to jump in the lake after school in the warm weather, listening to the people out on the water, and enjoying the beauty of it every day was peaceful.

For a while, everything was going well, and the kids were doing well in their new school, even though I'm sure they missed their other friends. Since I was still working nights at the nursing home in Augusta, I felt better being home during the day with the girls. The hard part was never getting enough sleep. I tried to sleep while the kids were at school, but found it very difficult to sleep during the day. I couldn't get used to sleeping in the daytime, and then on my days off back to sleeping nights, it was hard, but I did what I had to do. It was worth it though, to be home when the kids were home. My pregnancy was progressing without any complications. Jake was hoping for a boy and so was I, because I knew how pleased he would be. I hoped that a son would make all the difference for Jake and help him find some peace and happiness. I know, now, just how naive this was, because soon after moving into the lake house, Jake began making accusations that the baby I was carrying wasn't his.

He began saying I must have slept with someone else while he worked out of town. He'd sometimes pick up side jobs out of town, building a deck or redoing a kitchen. These jobs were usually for family members. Jake just couldn't help himself; he enjoyed making me feel guilty for something I didn't do, always to make himself feel better. Up to that point, I never imagined he would accuse me of this. What makes it even worse, he knew this baby was his, because if he didn't, he would never stay because then I wouldn't still be his "virgin," which I later learned was the whole reason why he married me.

Soon, I was going into labor. Boy, girl, I didn't care as long as I had a healthy baby. Jake only wanted a boy, and wouldn't shut up about how he would "carry on the Martin name." He was very excited, but why? I thought he believed the baby wasn't his? What a joke! Even as I'm writing this, the way he acted still infuriates me. I didn't realize until years later that his controlling behavior was because of his own weaknesses, and instead of working on himself and his issues, he took it out on me and the kids.

I don't remember how long I was in labor for, but when my baby was finally born, the doctor said,
  "It's a girl! She's beautiful!"
I was overjoyed. Until I heard Jake ask the doctor,
  "It's a boy, right? Are you sure it's not a boy?"
The doctor replied,
  "No, it's a girl."
I don't know how disappointed Jake felt inside, but he acted just as happy and excited as I was with her being a healthy girl. We named her "Marie Rose".

When we got home, it was like a switch had flipped. Jake started taking part in everything that Marie needed. He changed her diaper, fed her, and got up with her at night. I thought maybe he had finally grown up since his first two girls were born. He was now nine years older since Tara was born. Maybe he was more mature and realized he was missing out when he didn't do any of that for them. I couldn't be sure, but I knew that I was glad to see it and it gave me hope that maybe life was going to get better. Like this was going to change him. He was spending more time enjoying himself and not complaining, and Tara and Claire were enjoying their dad spending time with them. His focus was on their new baby sister Marie, but the girls were his big helpers, and he was being nicer to them, so they seemed happy. I still knew that things could change at any moment, and had to walk on eggshells, trying to keep everyone happy and hoping nothing set him off into a tirade of the smallest thing.

A couple of months after Marie was born, I needed to go back to work. Jake seemed fine, even knowing it meant he needed to get up at night with Marie. Of course, I knew Jake wanted me to get back to work and he knew I needed to feel safe leaving the baby alone with him so soon, so he acted different with Marie. I did not ask him about it; I just enjoyed it, hoping it would last forever. It was as if he was enjoying being a father for the first time, not acting like the kids were just a burden and a nuisance.

Sadly, it wasn't long before Jake started acting his usual self with me and the older girls. He would come home from work and want to spend time with Marie, but not Tara or Claire. They had to work for his attention. Something they did or didn't do always seemed to set him off. He'd always chastise one of them, expressing his disappointment in them not doing some task exactly as he pictured them doing it in his head. They would try to play with Marie, hoping to be a part of playtime with their dad, which was heartbreaking to watch, to see how hard they tried. They needed to know it wasn't anything they did; he was the problem. At that age, nothing you say is going to make them understand why their father showed them almost zero affection. For them to have to sit there and watch him play with their little sister while they were just cast aside like empty beer bottles, was traumatizing for them.

***

Tara and Claire always looked forward to summer because one of their friends, a young boy who lived out of state, would come up to Maine for the summer and they would hang out together. One afternoon, he came over to spend the day with the girls and they were so excited. Tara was eleven at the time and she and Claire couldn't wait to go swimming in the lake. They had on their adorable bathing suits. It was a hot sunny day out, so we were all sitting outside and the girls and their friend were down by the water getting ready to swim. Out of the blue, Jake yells over to Tara and says, "Hey Tara, you know you're getting chubby." I looked over at Tara and I could see the beautiful smile on her face disappear. You could see the joy drain from her face, as she was overcome with embarrassment. I yelled at Jake to stop and hoped that he would. I didn't want to make a big scene for fear that he would say more mean things about her. Tara tried to ignore him and go swimming with Claire and their friend, but I knew at that moment that what spirit she had inside had finally broken because of him. It was a hurtful blow to her self-esteem and her heart, but Jake didn't care. He enjoyed making others feel as terrible as possible. He wasn't a Father to them, but a cruel dictator.

To say something like that to his kids meant nothing to him, as long as he could put them down. He relished in that power to break someone's spirit. I know now just how much of a sociopath he was. He had no empathy or love for anyone but himself. He was just mean. Amazingly, to this day, after all the years of his abuse towards Tara, he acts as if he has no idea why, as an adult, she wants nothing to do with him and does not allow him to be around her children. In fact, these days, not a single one of our kids speaks to him, for everything he's put them through, but we'll get to that.

After that incident, I noticed a change in Tara. Now when she went to bed, she wouldn't kiss us goodnight anymore. I pointed it out to Jake, and his only reaction was "Well at her age she shouldn't be kissing me goodnight anyway, it's not right." Really? What an asshole. He always made excuses for everything he did. Could it be that she just hated him now and wanted nothing to do with him and hated me for not sticking up for her and leaving him?

As time passed, Jake's controlling behavior and cruelty to the kids and I only got worse. Like before, he started accusing me of cheating again. Not with anyone specific, as he had done before. This time it could have been with anyone. He was always obsessed with the fact that I was a virgin when we got together, like that's what he cared about the most. It drove him crazy, imagining I wanted to be with someone else because I had only been with him. He had convinced himself that one day I would be unfaithful, and his accusations would prove true. One afternoon, he was as sure as he's ever been that I cheated on him when we lived at the old camp. The kids and I had gone swimming with the next-door neighbor and his young son. Afterwards he and I went into the camp to get something cold to drink. I put on my terrycloth bathrobe because I was chilly and it was better than a big towel to cover me up. Not to mention that I'm very modest, and would never walk around in just my bathing suit. My terrycloth bathrobe hid everything. Almost as soon as we walked into the kitchen, Jake came walking in the house, and we all started making small talk. He said nothing of it in the moment. I didn't realize that in Jake's mind he thought I was up to something. He said that because we were inside; we were doing something shady.

After the neighbor left, Jake started accusing me of cheating. You would have thought I had my bathrobe on and nothing else underneath, the way he was acting, but that was, of course, not the case. He was so jealous that he couldn't think rationally. I didn't even realize that he was thinking this until the neighbor left. There was no reasoning with him since he was always going to assume the worst. I told him the truth and if he chose not to believe me, then that was his issue, not mine. I had nothing to feel guilty about.

I believe in marriage; I did not and do not believe in cheating during a marriage. If you want to be with someone else, then end the marriage. But I have to say, looking back now, sometimes I wish I had cheated on him. Jake was going to accuse me throughout my twenty-five years of marriage, anyways, so I should have done it. I remember hearing that if someone is accusing you of cheating, that's because they are the one cheating. I now wonder if this may have been true. Years after my marriage was over, I heard he had cheated with someone from our hometown. Who knows, and at this point, who cares? If he did, it didn't work out, most likely because of his own insecurities.

✳✳✳

After a couple of years, I started feeling concerned that Marie was growing up without a sibling closer to her in age. Tara and Claire were so much older. They grew up together. It made me sad to think that Marie wouldn't have that. I decided to have one more, knowing that Jake wanted another chance for a boy. I was adamant with Jake that he understood no matter what the sex of the baby, it was going to be my last child. I was only doing this for Marie, believing it was the right thing to do.

I wish I could say that this pregnancy was different; that Jake had some magical change of heart and was happy to have a family that loved him, and another child on the way to look forward to. I wish I could say that, but once again, during this pregnancy, Jake accused me of cheating, claiming that this baby was not his. He said that a friend of his told him I had cheated on him. Like a broken record, repeating the same lies just to torment me. What a sorry excuse for a man. It made me question what the hell I was doing bringing any more children into this situation. I had something seriously wrong with me if I would allow someone to treat me like this, especially when I knew he didn't believe what he was saying. He was just being cruel because he knew he could be. Sadly, this story would persist years later, where Jake never passed up an opportunity to tell my son that he was not Jake's child. I wish that was the worst of it. For now, I pushed these depressing thoughts out of my mind so I could just get through each day until the baby arrived.

This time it was "A Boy!" Oh, how happy his father was. Jake kissed me and thanked me for giving him a son. He cried, and I cried along with him. I never saw him like this. He finally had his son. We named him Shane Herbert Wilson; Herbert was to honor his grandfather and Wilson was his and his father's middle name. Now his family name would be passed on. I prayed to God that maybe this would be a changing moment in his life. Why wouldn't it be? Jake now had everything he ever asked for, a son. He would be so proud now. I gave him something he desperately wanted and suddenly, like a switch had flipped, he knew the baby was his. He never questioned my faithfulness again in those early years of Shane's development, but that wouldn't last. He now had a son to pass down his name, to be so proud of, to play football and baseball with. He now had three girls and a boy. Life doesn't get any better than this, right?

Just like with Marie, Jake was a very doting father to his new son, Shane. He changed him, fed him, held him and would also take turns getting up with him at night. He was just so happy. It was great for the girls because he was being nicer to all of them. The older girls would help a lot with keeping Marie entertained and helping with the baby. The girls were so excited that they were having some fun times with their father, even if it was because they played with Shane or Marie along with him. They needed their daddy time, even though I'm sure they knew It wasn't the same, but they would take whatever attention he would give them. It also thrilled them to have a little baby brother. They loved to play with him.

***

Before long, I had to go back to work again, still working the graveyard shift so I could be up all day with Marie and Shane and sleep a few hours in the evening before working all night. It was a lot, but you do what you must do.

We decided it was time to move out of this lake house, which had become far too small for a family of six. We only had two bedrooms, so we had no choice. Leaving was hard because I loved this home, being so beautiful, and I knew it would never be ours again.

Chapter

3

Living In Fear

Jake had finished building our new house in the town of Windsor, just enough so we could live there while he finished the rest of the interior. It was a nice cape-style house. I had always wanted a Cape because they are such nice country-style homes. The chalet-style home was beautiful on the lake or with a mountain view, but a cape fits in anywhere in the country. I was excited to have this house, which Jake told us was going to be our family home. It was on five acres of land on a private road with access to a lake. It was a perfect place to raise our kids.

Unfortunately, Jake couldn't pass up the opportunity to let us down again. Once we moved in, he let me know that he had every intention of selling this house. It was going to be temporary, not our forever home. He wouldn't allow us to hang pictures on the walls because he didn't want any nail holes, even though he could have just spackled them when the time came. The kids couldn't even fix up their rooms, to make it their own. They could have a bed, dresser and nightstand, nothing on the walls, no posters or paint. He refused to finish the floors until we were moving out, so the house could be perfect for the new homeowners. We should have been the new homeowners, but he never thought about what we wanted. It didn't matter to him that for us it was just plywood. I never understood how a father, a carpenter who built homes for a living, would not build a home for his own family. He said to me, "We don't need our own home; we are just going to keep building and moving." He knew, from a conversation I had with him about my childhood, that the one thing I hated was moving around so many times as a child. We had to move at least eight times and had to switch schools several times. I did not want that for our children. I believe that is why it gave him such pleasure to tell me he had no intention of building us a permanent home. I tried to enjoy living there despite my deep disappointment.

About a quarter mile down the road from our house, Jake had built another split-foyer home that my sister ended up buying. She had recently become widowed and moved up from New York. It was nice having her and her kids next door. My girls loved having their cousins nearby. They could walk to the school bus together at the end of the road and play together after school. Of course, my sister and I both worked full-time, so we didn't see each other too often, but often enough. My mother was living with my sister, too, helping her take care of the kids. I wasn't sure how long we would end up staying in this house, but I would make the most of it in the meantime. I was still working as a nurse's assistant but had left the nursing home in Augusta for a job a few miles from home. I still had to work the graveyard shift because they didn't have any day shift positions available. As soon as they did, with the kids getting older, I was going to switch to days so I could be home in the evenings with the kids. In the meantime, Tara and Claire had no choice but to watch their younger siblings so I could get a few hours of sleep before going to work. Their father had no intention of helping with the childcare after his workday was done. Nothing changed with Jake. He would just come home, eat his dinner, drink his beer, watch TV and yell at the kids for whatever he believed they did wrong. Tara and Claire couldn't have play dates with friends, join in any after-school activities or spend time with their cousins after school because they had to watch Shane and Marie so I could sleep for a few hours before work.

***

I found out years later, when my kids were adults, that while I was asleep things were bad. My daughter, Claire, has permanent damage to her hands because her father would make her wash the dishes in scalding-hot water because, he said, the dishes would not be clean enough. He would yell at her if it wasn't hot enough and stand there to make sure it was red hot and painful to the touch. I never knew this, but would that have changed anything? Probably not. I had to sleep at least a few hours so I could function at work. I was lucky if I could sleep 4-5 hours each night. I started working 12 and 16-hour shifts five days a week just to pay for groceries and health insurance for all of us and would have to leave for work right after dinner. I'm ashamed to admit that every night, I hoped that Jake drank enough beer so he would pass out and not bother the kids. It worked some nights, but not enough.

I also learned that Tara and Claire resented having to watch their younger siblings when I had to sleep or leave for work early. They would sometimes lock Marie and Shane out of the house and throw toilet paper out to them if they said they had to go to the bathroom. Who knows what else they did? As adults, they have expressed to me how unfair it was that they had to watch them. I agree. It wasn't fair for them to be robbed of their childhood by having to care for their siblings but what else could I have done? Their father did not watch them, and I had to work. I believe most siblings have some unhappy memories, but for my kids it was just another unhappy memory among so many unhappy memories.

Eventually, a day shift position opened, and I decided that no matter what, I was taking this position. I paid for Shane to go to daycare and Marie to go to after-school daycare, if needed. It meant I could be home in the evenings and the kids didn't have to worry anymore about being alone with their father. Some days I worked late, but most days I was home by four o'clock. I knew this would be better for Jake too, because he couldn't stand that I had to sleep in the evenings and would wake me up after only a few hours' sleep believing that 3 or 4 hours was enough sleep for me to work the entire night. This coming from a man who slept a full eight hours each night before work. I believe he wanted company while he watched his TV shows so he had someone to complain to about what he was watching, if that makes sense.

Jake always watched the show, "Fleecing of America". This television show and others like it made him so mad every time he watched them, but he had to watch them anyway. He would say "I love this show" and then start bitching and complaining about the topic of the night's show. He would get so angry about it. It was a vicious cycle with these shows. I couldn't figure out why he watched these shows if they upset him so much, but now I realize it's because he enjoyed getting mad. It's hard to understand the thinking behind this, and unfortunately, we were the ones who had to bear the brunt of it.

I used to watch the show "Roseanne", which I enjoyed because it was hilarious. Unsurprisingly, Jake hated it. He would say that, because the character, Roseanne, was the boss of her family, it was "bullshit" and "who the hell did she think she was?" It was just a TV show. The fact that I liked the show didn't matter, if he didn't approve of it, he didn't want to see it on our TV. Now, thinking back at some things he would get so mad about, it was ridiculous. If I was enjoying something that he had an issue with, he would get so angry that I would have to shut it off just to shut him up. If I was listening to a Billy Joel song, he would say to me, "You're listening to him just to piss me off. There's no way you like his music!" He then continued his rant with "How does someone that ugly get someone so beautiful like Christy Brinkley? Obviously, she only married him for his money." He was always so jealous. Jealous of everybody. If Billy Joel came on the radio while we were driving in the car, he would insist on switching the station.

I cannot remember every day or every moment in this house. I have repressed a lot for many years, and now it's hard to remember every detail. As I am writing this book, I have forced myself to think about these years and to recall these unhappy memories. Some were much worse than the usual bad times. Sadly, there were so few happy memories. The best times in my life were when each of my children were born, but in our house, we all walked on eggshells. The greatest times and memories for my children and I were when we got together with my family. I would take the kids every so often to visit my family and, in the summers, we went camping for many years with all of them. All the aunts, uncles and cousins would go, and we would have a great time. Their grandma would be there too. The kids had so much fun. Not one time did Jake come camping with us, thank God. In all the years we went, he couldn't imagine having family time with his kids and maybe actually having a good time. He could have gone fishing with his son, swimming with his daughters, roasting marshmallows over the fire with his family, but NO, not him. Those weren't worth his time. His children weren't worth his time. I'd try to talk him into coming with us, even for a couple of days, but he never would. Now that I think back to it, I'm thankful he never came with us. I am sure he would have ruined it, got into an argument with someone and forbid us from ever going again.

For years, Jake promised the kids that he would take them to Disney World. He started saying this when Tara and Claire were little, which never happened, and then he promised the same thing years later to Marie and Shane, which also never happened. He would tell them, and then use some bullshit reason for why he refuses to take them, like if they didn't do something exactly as he pictured them doing it. One year, he told Shane to shovel the snow out of our driveway. Jake immediately had a problem because Shane didn't shovel as fast as Jake expected him to do it, and that would then become a reason why Jake wouldn't take the kids to Disney. It wasn't that Shane wasn't shoveling snow, but that he didn't "hustle", according to Jake. I can remember one year, Jake didn't want me to take the kids on my family's camping trip, so he lied to me and said that he wanted to take the kids on vacation somewhere special. Jake knew how badly I wanted him to do just that, but then he told me that the only way he'd do that was if I didn't go on the camping trip. I knew he was up to something. Of course, I knew he would not keep his word, and this promised trip would never happen, so the kids and I went camping and had a great time like we did every year.

I talked to Jake about planning a family vacation. I pointed out that we had done nothing together with the kids and, before we knew it, they'd be grown, and the opportunity would be gone. I knew he would never pay for a trip, so I told him I would plan it and pay for everything if he promised to do this for them. He agreed, and said, "Ok, as long as you're paying for it."

I planned a trip to Six Flags. I knew the kids would be excited to go there and, while it may not be Disney World, it was a place that had fun rides and water parks and was close enough to home so Jake would travel there. After telling the kids, they were as excited as I hoped they would be. I think they were shocked that this was going to happen. Of course, they didn't know that their dad wasn't paying for any of it; that I was paying for him to act like a proper father who wanted to spend time with his kids and have fun with them. I was just hoping he might have fun with them, and they would see that.

We went for two days and one night. I reserved a suite, so it had two separate bedrooms, a kitchen and a living room. It was a nice room with plenty of space for all of us. The kids were thrilled when we got to the hotel. How could they not be, it was a real vacation trip together, something we'd never done before. They enjoyed the idea of getting room service and being able to just have fun.

We checked out the room and decided who would sleep where, before going down to the park. It was very exciting to see the kids so happy and their father acting happy too. I could see a true glimmer of happiness in Shane's smile, being there with his dad, looking so forward to spending time with him and having fun.

Without all the details, I can say the first day was a great day. Jake was in a good mood, and the kids were having a great time. He was going on the rides with them and seemed to be enjoying himself. I was having a great time just watching them laughing and having fun together. I did not go on rides myself because of my fear of heights but enjoyed taking pictures of them and just walking around and seeing everything.

We had lunch at the park and would have dinner back at the hotel when we returned. Anything the kids wanted; I wanted them to have. They deserved to have the best vacation ever. We posed for a family picture that they took at the park, and I still have it, even though it doesn't hold any fond memories. I still treasure it as the one family vacation we ever took together. I had hoped this trip would lead to more family trips in the future but, unfortunately, it did not.

The second day proved that Jake could only stand having fun with the kids for one day. I guess that was all he could muster after all these years. I could see that they were now getting on his nerves, and he stated that he shouldn't have taken two days off from work. That comment was a bad sign. We went down to the park and Jake was very impatient, especially with Shane. It seemed that anything Shane did or said made him mad. The older girls were able to walk ahead of us, so they didn't have to listen to their fathers' complaints. I could still see them to make sure they were safe, but I wanted to allow them a little escape. Marie chose to stay behind with us, I believe to make sure Shane was okay. She was very protective of her brother and tried to be a buffer between him and his dad any way she could.

It came to a boiling point when they were going on a water ride and Shane was afraid to do it. Jake knew how frightened he was but insisted he do it anyway. He began yelling at Shane, not caring that we were around all these other people. Jake was making a scene and embarrassing all of us. It's not like Shane hadn't gone on all the other rides, but this water ride was too scary for him, and he was only about five years old. I think the more afraid Shane was, the more Jake enjoyed it and wasn't going to let up until he did it. He started screaming at him even more. At this point, Shane was crying, begging not to have to do it. Unfortunately, they were already in the middle of the line, which was in waist-high water, approaching the water ride, so Shane was out of my reach. I couldn't get to him and take him out of there. His father would have needed to take him out of the water. It was a tubing water ride on level ground then it had a big drop off and that's what frightened Shane so much. It was possible to not have to go down it, but Jake was not going to let that happen. I yelled to Jake and told him not to make him do this, but he didn't care, he was going to make him no matter what any of us were saying.

Finally, the ride was over and poor Shane was so upset and shaken up over this. It was obvious now that no one was having fun anymore. The girls became visibly upset by the whole thing. From that moment on, there was no more laughter coming from them as they walked around the park. Even the way they carried themselves had changed. There was no more excitement. Their dad had ruined the fun and now they only worried about when he would get angry at Shane, again, or maybe one of them. Shane was not enjoying himself anymore. He just stayed with me and walked around, before we ended up leaving the park early that day, heading home much earlier than we were planning on. Of course, that was fine with Jake. Now looking back, I'm sure that's what he was hoping for. He had said more than once "I should have worked today."

What a shame that he couldn't even enjoy two full days with his kids without his anger reappearing and seeing the obvious resentment he had towards us for having to be there. Two days was all I asked of him, and it didn't cost him a thing except good memories that his kids could have remembered for a lifetime. Without fail, his cruelty always casts a shadow on any happy times.

As an adult, Shane once told me that he can't remember a single happy moment he has ever had with his father. Not one. This was just another disappointment along with all the other disappointments, but I always hoped that the next time might be different. Foolish me. I realize now how futile it was to always hope that things would change. I ask myself, "Why didn't I give up hope after each disappointment? "I just kept thinking something would make Jake change one day. I thought he would act differently towards his son, the boy he couldn't wait for. I hoped Jake would realize that he could have a loving family and a great life if he would just accept us the way we were. I loved him and the children loved him. All we wanted from him was his approval and for his constant anger and meanness to diminish. How did Jake not realize that his kids would grow up resenting him for his actions, much the same way he resented his own father? That's the irony. Jake hated his father and had nothing to do with him until the man was dying. And yet, Jake followed in his father's footsteps. True to form, none of my kids speak with him, now. On the other hand, how did I not realize that what I was doing to my kids; how subjecting them to an angry and mean father would also cause them to eventually resent me as well? Neither of us realized the long-term consequences of our actions. He didn't care and I was afraid to leave him.

It is sad when all your memories are so negative, and you must struggle to find any positive ones. Sometimes I can remember just watching a comedy show on TV and laughing along with Jake, first because they were funny, and second because he was in a good mood, and I wanted to do anything to keep him that way. I'm sure we had a few other times that were okay, but if they started out fun, they almost always ended badly, and weren't good memories. Jake could only act happy for short periods of time before something I or someone else said or did just set him off into a fit of anger. His anger would come on so suddenly, especially if his kids showed any emotions, Shane in particular. One afternoon, after traveling nowhere in particular, Jake opened a car door to let Shane out (child locks meant he couldn't open the door.) As Shane was climbing out of his booster seat and wasn't yet out of the car, Jake slammed the car door directly onto Shane's hand. He couldn't have been more than 5 or 6 years old. Shane immediately erupted in tears and held his hurt hand. What did Jake do? He grabbed Shane, shaking him violently while screaming at him through gritted teeth to stop crying, or Jake would "give him something to cry about." As if he hadn't just done that, already. Shane immediately stopped crying, fighting back tears, out of fear his father would hurt him worse than he just had.

For so many years I thought it was alcohol that had made Jake this way, and it's not like I never drank. When we moved to Maine, his sister introduced me to a coffee brandy drink, which I enjoyed, so I had my fair share of drinks, though not nightly like him, but on some of my nights off. Eventually I learned that, though the beer might make it worse, even when he wasn't drinking, he was still angry and mean. There are so many terrible memories in that house on Smith Road that I don't even know where to begin. And he wasn't drunk for some of the worst ones.

Jake always enjoyed telling me what he would do to me if I ever tried to leave him. We would be sitting in the kitchen, and he would say "If you ever try to leave me, I will shoot you and bury you out back where no one would ever find you." The scary thing is that he wasn't joking; I believed that he would hurt me. He loved watching those true-crime murder shows and always commented on how they got caught because they did this wrong and that wrong. Forensic Files, Cold Case Files, etc. were some of his favorite shows. He mentioned it so much that I wrote a letter stating that if something happened to me, that I didn't just leave, but that Jake killed me and buried me somewhere out back of the house. I wrote it just in case his threats ever became a reality.

He enjoyed making fun of my insecurities and made sure I never felt good about myself. Even the little insults would cut me like a knife. I don't know how or why I still loved this man. What was it going to take for me to stop loving him and start hating him? I knew I could never leave him, but I still didn't have to let his comments and insults hurt me as much as they did. I should have turned to stone and not cared about what he said or did to me, but that was not the case.

One time when I got home from work, Jake started laughing at me for some strange reason. Then he said, "I just passed you on the road and you looked so stupid!" imitating what I looked like. Apparently, while on his way to get cigarettes or beer, he had passed me on the road as I was heading home from work and saw me singing along with the radio like most people do, including Jake himself. I don't even think I responded, it just hurt. I could feel this overwhelming feeling coming over me, like cutting off my air as another piece of my heart was being chipped away. What a fool I was to let him make me feel this way, but I wasn't about to let him see how much it bothered me. I just ignored him and started making dinner, even though inside, it hurt. There were many times I didn't care whether I lived or died, but I was always afraid that if something happened to me, my kids' lives with him would be even worse. That was my biggest fear. Them being left alone with Jake. I could not let that happen. It was bad enough that I continued to stay with him, but at least they had me too. Sometimes, the thought of us both not being there sounded good to me.

There is one instance at this home that made me feel this way. Jake had not been feeling well, feeling tired, and had lost some weight without even trying. He was getting concerned because there was a new health scare out there called HIV and Aids. Jake had a blood transfusion around 1979 after being hit by a car while riding on his bike, before I met him, and they had mentioned on the news that some blood used for transfusions was tainted with this disease. I don't believe Jake would have given it a second thought, except he worried about why he wasn't feeling well. He went to the doctor to have an HIV test done, which takes a few days to get the results.

At this point, Jake had convinced himself that he had HIV and was going to die. At the time, this disease sounded like a death sentence. Many people were dying from it before medications to treat it became available. Having worked with Aids patients myself, I saw firsthand that their prognosis was not very hopeful. Jake said that his biggest fear was that he would die, and I would live and enjoy life without him. I can recall him saying, "You'll be happy living with some other man." He was not about to let that happen. The next thing I remember is him pulling me down the hallway towards our bedroom saying, "If I'm going to die, then so are you." He was going to rape me, giving me the disease, which he was convinced he had, so I could die too.

At first, I remember fighting back, trying to push him away, then off me, but of course he was stronger than me, so it was impossible. In that moment, he was so mad that his anger made him even stronger. I don't remember if I was crying or not, I remember laying there thinking, "I give up, why bother fighting back when there's no hope? Maybe the kids will be better off if we're both dead. At least they will be free from their abusive father, and as long as I'm alive, he's never going to let me go. The kids are better off with my family than with us." I also didn't know at the time that it was considered rape if your husband forced you to have sex. This wasn't just rape; it was attempted murder, really. At that moment, he wanted me to die like he was convinced he was going to die.

I didn't realize I had a say in anything when it came to my marriage. This is not an excuse, just a fact, I didn't know. You could say I was stupid and naïve. I did not have role models who showed me that women can be strong, that we are important, that we matter when it comes to anything besides being a wife, housekeeper, mother, working full time and anything else your husband wants you to do. Growing up, my sisters and I were raised not to stand up for ourselves. We didn't have a role model for a healthy marriage. My father had left my mother when I was very young, and my mother, left alone with six children, had to bend to the wishes of my grandparents. They bossed her around and she never stood up to them. She was expected to be docile, sweet and obedient, and so were her six children. If an adult (aunts, uncles, grandparents, teachers) put you down or made fun of you, which happened a lot as a kid, we had to take it. I never had a backbone, I never learned how to stand up for myself. Even at my age now, standing up to someone who is mistreating me in any way is almost unbearable. I'm embarrassed to admit this, but it's true. I constantly say to my kids now, "Please learn from my mistakes." It's the only advice I have for them. Don't let anyone treat you badly and make you feel worthless, belittled, and scared. How stupid and naïve I really was, but the question is, "Would it have mattered, would it have changed anything that happened?" I will never know. In the end, Jake's HIV test came back negative, he was not sick at all. What I don't understand is how I just repressed this event and went on like it never happened. The next day I just continued with this outward image of living a happy life, just as I had always done.

As time went on, it got harder on the kids. Tara and Claire were in high school, which brought on other challenges for them besides the ones at home. It seemed especially hard for Tara. Jake always found pleasure in making fun of his kids' appearance. For example, he knew Claire was very self-conscious of her nose, so he started calling her Toucan Sam, which was very upsetting to her. It made her feel worse, and he knew that. Tara would have a bout of acne, so he would call her pizza face, and Marie thought she had a large forehead so he would hold his own hair back on his forehead and say, "Who do I look like?" I just don't understand how a father would find such joy in making fun of his kids and want them to feel bad about themselves. It seemed to give Jake great satisfaction. He would just laugh and laugh and say, "I'm just joking with you, why don't you laugh?" I would explain to him that it's not funny if the jokes are solely at their expense. Yet, there I was, always forgiving him for his terrible treatment of them.

For many years I didn't know it was abuse. Yelling wasn't abuse, was it? He wasn't hitting the kids like he was hit as a child, or so I thought. He used to say to me, "I'm not hitting them, I'm only yelling. They have no idea what I went through." He wasn't hitting me either. He always had excuses and so did I. I used to think, poor Jake, he doesn't mean to do it. He had such an awful childhood with his dad, so it could be much worse. If I remember all the times I felt sorry for him, I could just scream!!

I kept making excuses and expecting the kids not to fear Jake's yelling. He wasn't hitting them, after all, though he constantly threatened them. He had been beaten by his dad on numerous occasions. Sometimes his dad would just walk by him and back-hand smack him for no reason. I never heard of verbal or emotional abuse, only physical abuse. I didn't realize the damage that verbal and emotional abuse can do. I believe now that it is even worse than physical abuse. As time went on, I used to wish Jake would hit me, just so other people could see what he was doing to us, and I would have a reason to leave him that was obvious to those on the outside.

Tara rebelled against her dad in the only way she knew how to. At the time, I wasn't happy about it because it just brought more stress in the home, but I understand why she did it. It was the only way she could stand up to him and control this part of her life. For instance, she wanted to get her nose pierced and Jake said, absolutely not. He was against body piercing and tattoos. He always said, "When you're 18 and not living in my house, then you can do what you want, but not while you're living in my house."

So, one night Tara slept over at a friend's house, and I picked her up after school the next day. When I arrived at her high school, I saw Tara walking towards my car with my old "m.a.s.h." t-shirt on and green camouflage pants. Her blonde hair had been dyed green and her nose was pierced. It shocked me. I didn't know what I was going to do, I just knew this was going to turn into a huge fight at home and that worried me. I would try at all costs to prevent fights, if possible, but Tara was ready and willing for an all-out blow-up. I know now that she decided she was going to fight back in the only way she knew, and if her dad was going to yell at her anyway, she was going to give him reasons for doing it. If you think about it, it was very smart of her, her wanting to get back at him for all the hurt he had caused her. She knew this would hurt him by purposely not listening to him and making him angry. Brilliant actually, but very scary at the same time.

I was not happy; I don't know exactly what I said to Tara, but I'm sure I yelled and said how angry her father was going to be when we got home. How could she do this to us? I know that I told her to take that ring out of her nose and to wash that green out of her hair. Luckily it was just a wash-in, so after a few shampoos it came out. Besides, this was not just going to affect her; this was going to affect all of us. Any time he was mad at the kids, it was always my fault. Honestly, I cannot remember what happened when Jake got home, but I know it wasn't good and obviously I blocked it out because it didn't go well. But this was not the end. Tara found other ways to make her father angry.

The next time Jake was yelling at her for who knows what reason, he threatened to hit her, which was a new thing he would say to all the kids. It was always a threat, and you never knew if it would turn into physical abuse. You always felt the tension and we knew he wanted to do it, it was only a matter of time before it happened. He even raised his hand like he was going to strike you. You never knew when or if that line would be crossed. But Tara had decided she would not allow that to happen to her anymore. She decided she would stand up to him and speak back, and so she did.

I can see him yelling at her and suddenly, I hear Tara yelling back at him saying "If you even dare to hit me, I will report you so fast to the school and the authorities." It shocked me! I could see the rage in her dad's face, now beat red with anger. I can't even quote word for word what they said, but Tara won that argument. She had put her dad in his place and that made him crazy. How dare one of his kids speak back to him and threaten him.

It was the bravest and smartest thing Tara ever did for herself against him, at that point in her life, anyway. Why couldn't I do that? Why couldn't I threaten him just like he threatened me? I guess because I was a coward.

One day Tara came to me and asked if she could please paint a drawing on her bedroom wall. She wanted it to be something special to make her room more bearable. I know her bedroom was boring without being allowed to hang posters on the walls like a normal teenager gets to, and that is where she spent most of her time when she was home. As far away from her dad as possible. I let her paint just one wall. What could it hurt, it's just paint and can be repainted when we move, right? What's the worst that can happen? Jake will yell, but he's going to yell about something anyway, so I said it was okay.

Tara was very excited and couldn't wait to get started. She loved to draw and paint pictures. I did not know what she was going to paint, but it was her room, so I wasn't worried about that. She would draw it out first and then paint it. It took several days to finish it, but her dad hardly ever went upstairs. He rarely ever went up to any of the girl's rooms. If he wanted them, he would just yell and tell them to come down. I don't remember what she drew at this point in my memory, but I believe I have a picture of it somewhere. I know it was nice, and she only did the one wall like I had said. I also knew that once I gave Tara permission, her sisters Marie and Claire would want to do it in their rooms too, which was only fair. Claire let her friends write all over her wall. It was not a nice, simple picture. It was not attractive, but she liked it.

I don't know how long it was before Jake discovered Tara's wall, but one night, he went up to her room upset of course about something, and then it happened. He saw the wall. He started screaming at her. I ran up the stairs to make sure she didn't get blamed. I don't remember the exact words, but I told him that I gave Tara permission, and it was not a big deal to paint the wall white again before we sold it. He then walked into the other girls' rooms, saw their drawings on their walls, and started yelling. It was ridiculous, I thought. I think he was even angrier that I let her do it, knowing he would never have allowed it and how dare I allow it behind his back. I told him that I thought it would be nice for Tara to express herself in a positive, creative way. I guess I had a moment of "backbone" and I only wish it had continued.

Tara was having a rough time dealing with every-thing going on in her life. She was being mistreated by her father, dealing with a mother who let it happen, and then I later learned she was dealing with bullying at school. I learned from Claire that Tara was being bullied at school because she had started dating girls, and her classmates did not accept it well. Previously, Tara had dated boys, but they did nothing but hurt her, so she must have decided they were all bad and didn't want to deal with them. I had no idea that Tara liked girls. It was surprising news to me, and I know that when Tara told me, I did not handle it very well. I accused her of just doing it for attention. I am not proud of that, and I truly regret my reaction. It wasn't just for attention, as I later learned. I wasn't against anyone being gay, because I believe you like who you like, I just didn't understand why Tara changed, but then I also didn't know that she had some traumatic events happen to her because of some boy which I will not write about.

My biggest concern was the reaction from Jake when he heard that Tara was dating girls. I believe that's what I was actually reacting to. I would be the one who would have to hear him rant about it along with everything else he believed Tara ever did wrong. I knew he could go on for weeks about the same things, over and over, as if it did any good. Jake would always say, "It's your fault and you need to talk to her and straighten her out." He thought that somehow, I could get Tara or the other kids to listen to what he wanted and expected. It always had to be someone else's fault, because he believed none of their issues were ever his fault.

Eventually everything became too difficult for Tara to bear, and she became depressed. I guess, how could you not be with all this happening in your life. One day I received a call from the high school principal telling me that Tara was suicidal and that they were sending her by ambulance to a psychiatric hospital in Waterville. I was horrified that it had come to this point. How the hell did I not realize that something like this could happen?

I called Jake, and we headed to the hospital as soon as possible. Jake was not happy and believed this was just another stunt of Tara's. Jake did not believe in any mental issues, didn't believe in therapy, or in telling anyone else your business. He believed that any issues our children had, whether emotional or mental, came from my side of the family. He always said, "They didn't get that from my side of the family."

After we arrived at the hospital, we walked inside, where someone greeted us at the door and took us into an office to tell us what happened. They said Tara told someone at school that she was thinking of killing herself and how she might do it. I remember, my heart just sank, and all I could think about was how she could say such a thing. Was life really that bad? How did I not realize that, yes, life is that bad, and it depressed her?

Tara started crying and pleading with us not to leave her there. She promised she wouldn't harm herself and to please take her home. It was the hardest decision I ever had to make. Jake would have let her come home just so we could pretend this never happened. He didn't like anyone knowing our business, and then wouldn't have to worry about what she might tell them about her home life. I couldn't do that, nor did I care what she told them. We needed to do what was best for Tara, and that was for her to get the help she needed. She needed to talk to someone about everything that was going on in her life. It would also benefit her having time away from her father. We needed to admit her against her will, and we did.

After a few days, they allowed us to come and visit her. We didn't get to go to Tara's room; we had to visit her in a large rec room where there were several tables and chairs. They brought us in there to see Tara along with other family members visiting their loved ones. You didn't have any privacy, but I suppose no one else cared about your issues. They were dealing with their own. Tara acted happy to see us, which was a relief to me, and thanked me for making her stay. I didn't know what to expect after having to leave her here. During another visit, Tara asked us to join her in family counseling where she could say whatever she needed to say to her dad and myself. Jake was not comfortable with it, but he didn't have a choice. As hard as it would be for Tara, and for us to hear it, it was necessary for her recovery. I can remember sitting next to Jake, feeling nervous that he might get defensive when Tara tried to talk, but I remember he just sat there as she spoke, and he didn't utter a word. When we left the room, I could feel the steam coming off of him and once we got into the car, he ranted about everything he didn't agree with. I couldn't help but enjoy a sense of satisfaction that he had to listen to her.

I believe Tara was there for two or three weeks. It could have been longer, but I cannot be sure. I cannot remember a lot of details about a lot of these events. I know things at home were no different and unfortunately it was just a temporary fix for Tara. I don't even recall them having Tara receive outpatient therapy, and I realize now that it was necessary for her. Jake never owned up to anything Tara said he did, and that of course did not help at all.

Tara and Claire were at odds with each other much of the time for reasons I was unaware of at the time. Claire was very "moody" as a young girl and Tara was a bit more passive. Much later, I found out that Tara was disgusted with Claire because she thought Claire was such a suck-up to their father. Claire would do everything her dad told her to do, and Tara thought she was trying to be a "goody-two-shoes." Tara endured more insults from her father than Claire did because of her different build from Claire. Jake criticized Tara's curvy build. Tara also suffered from being well-endowed, and men stared at her not caring that she was a child, not an adult. It made her uncomfortable. One time, I had to yell at some man while I was pumping gas because he wouldn't stop staring at Tara's chest, saying, "She's only 14!" Of course, that embarrassed him, and he looked away. I am sure I embarrassed Tara as well, but I couldn't stand it. It was disgusting and unfair. What the hell was wrong with people?

I can remember one instance when Claire came crying to me, saying that Tara had chased her around the house with a knife while I was sleeping. I laid down for a few hours while they watched Shane and Marie. I was still working the night shift at that time. Claire was crying so hard, shaking and scared. I couldn't believe what she was saying. What was I going to do? I had to go to work and just pray that nothing would happen. I didn't believe that Tara would have hurt Claire, but just wanted to scare Claire and get revenge on her. I knew I needed to go to work soon and, when I told their father about what happened, he just brushed it off and thought it was ridiculous. What I should have done was not go to work and let Claire know she was safe. I can't even recall what I said to Tara about the whole incident. I should have sat them both down and tried to talk to them about it, but I'm sure I didn't. There's no excuse for that.

Claire had her own way of being mean to Tara, too, by making her feel bad about her size. Claire flaunted her ability to go into cool stores and buy cute little tops that didn't come in Tara's size. Things like that. Claire would make fun of Tara and wasn't very nice to her. They both had their way of hurting each other. They didn't realize that they each were doing what they had to do to make their lives more bearable. Claire did everything Jake told her to because he frightened her. She was nervous about what he might do if she didn't do everything perfectly. Tara rebelled against him, because of his seeming preference for Claire and his extra meanness towards Tara. We were all caught up in it but couldn't see the patterns of dysfunctional behaviors that arose from Jake's toxic behavior. We were each trying to get through every day as best we could. No day was without stress when Jake was around.

Soon after that knife incident, Tara ended up back in the hospital. This time, she was signing herself in because she knew she needed help. I believe it worried her that she might hurt herself or someone else. Once we arrived at the Emergency Room, Tara changed her mind and didn't want to stay, but I knew she had felt she needed to be there. Because Tara was a minor, it was up to me and for her sake, I once again signed her in against her will. It is so hard to have your child begging you to let them go home and you have to leave them there. As I am writing this, it is hard to come to grips with the fact that I didn't leave Jake and provide a more peaceful existence for my children. I was afraid of Jake, and I didn't believe I could leave him. I was convinced he would kidnap the kids and take off for a wilderness area where I couldn't find him. That's what Jake told me he would do, and I didn't doubt it. Once again, Tara's hospital stay was just a temporary fix for a serious problem.

So many incidents happened I should be ashamed of. Even though Tara and Claire had different things going on at home, they both suffered. Once, while Claire was riding her bike, she flew over the handlebars and hurt herself. She came home crying hysterically and had obviously hurt her collarbone and shoulder. Jake was annoyed that she hurt herself and didn't want her to ask to go to the doctor. He would not allow me to take her to the hospital, because it would cost too much, and he didn't believe she needed to go. I can't believe I listened to him, but that was what I did, so I never took her to the doctor. I knew she was hurt seriously, but I also believed that it was one of those types of injuries that they couldn't do anything about except put a sling on her arm to keep her collarbone in the right place. Sort of like breaking ribs, where they just wrap them but can't do anything else. Her collarbone was sticking out further on one side and never went back into place, and now she suffers with flare-ups and pain off and on, because the collarbone fused to her shoulder bone and didn't heal correctly. That is my fault.

Tara and Claire would have ear infections since they were very young, and Jake never wanted me to take them to the doctor. He would say "I had them as a child and my father never allowed me to go, I just had to suffer through it." But then in his next breath he would say, "That's why I have hearing loss and ruptured my ear drum more than once." Nevertheless, I wasn't about to let them suffer and possibly lose their hearing because he cared only about the money. I took them to the doctor despite his objections.

Claire was always self-conscious of her teeth, which were quite crooked. She would never smile in pictures because of it, so my mother offered to pay for Claire to get braces, which was so generous and sweet. However, Jake refused. He believed it would make him look bad if my mother paid for them, yet he had no intention of ever paying for them himself. So, of course, Claire did not get braces. If it wasn't for me and my dental insurance, the kids would never have been able to get regular dental care. I made sure they always went twice a year for their cleanings while I had insurance. The times that I didn't have insurance, Jake would not let me take them to the dentist and spend the money. Money was always a priority, not the kids or me.

Another thing Claire would have to deal with for many years was Bronchitis in the winters. She would start to dread winters just knowing that, once again, she would get it and have to listen to her father yelling at her when she coughed, as if she could control it or as if it was her fault. Jake would get so angry if he heard her coughing at night while he was trying to sleep. He would yell to her "Cough into your pillow," without any concern for her. Night after night, we would all have to listen to him get mad and yell at her over this. It was terrible. She could not control it and the medicine didn't help with the cough, especially at night. To have to be yelled at because you are sick is just wrong. When Jake was sick, he would expect us to feel bad for him, but if any of us were sick, he just wanted us out of his sight. You were no good to him that way, and he didn't want to see you or hear you. Again, we just had to endure his mistreatment.

Tara was about to graduate high school, and Jake wanted to sell the house and move as soon as graduation was over. Jake finally realized that he couldn't make money building homes in Maine. He decided he wanted to work on million-dollar homes in New York, on the east coast of Long Island, in the Hamptons. I was surprised because that meant moving back near my family. Like I always say, with Jake, money talks. He didn't think of all the other stuff that was going to get on his nerves in the near and dreaded future.

Tara was not going to move with us, of course, and I didn't really expect her to. I certainly understood why she would want to get away from us. Who could blame her? Claire was happy at first with the idea of moving. I was relieved that she was so positive about it, because I knew what it was like to have to move as a junior in high school and the challenges that go with that. When you're moving from a very small school to a very large one, it can be a difficult adjustment. Claire liked Long Island and thought it would be better than living in the rural boonies of Maine. I believe she loved the idea of all the stores and shops being so close by, some even within walking distance. Unfortunately, as the time drew closer, Claire was starting to have second thoughts because now it was sinking in that she would miss her friends, and everything would be different. It was beginning to be scary, but unfortunately, it was going to happen anyway, so she was going to have to find a way to make it good.

Chapter

4

From Fear To Hell

Jake rented the upstairs part of a house for us in Huntington Station, NY. It was a split-level home and someone else rented out the basement apartment which included the backyard access. On Long Island, having access to a backyard was not as big a deal, because there was so much they could do. They could ride bikes on the sidewalks, play in the front yard, and they would meet some kids and be able to play in their yards, plus they would have fun playing with their cousins when we visited.

As you entered the front door, there was a set of stairs leading straight up into a small hallway. At the top of the stairs, to the right, was the living room. It was a nice size and had a large window, which was great because it brought in a lot of sunlight. To the left and around the corner, was a good-sized eat-in-kitchen that fit a large table so there was plenty of room for us to eat in there. Across from the kitchen, the hallway led to the bedrooms. Our bedroom was the first door on the left, and halfway down the long hall on the left was Shane's bedroom. It was a small room, so we put bunk beds in there. This way, if he had a cousin sleepover, then we would have an extra bed. The next door was the bathroom, and further down was Marie and Claire's bedroom that they shared. I remember little about their bedroom; however, Shane's bedroom stands out like a bad memory. I could picture his bed, the size of his room, and where his toys were, but there was a reason for that. His room is where I spent a lot of nights consoling him after a bad time at home.

The house we lived in wasn't in the greatest area, but it could have been a lot worse. We weren't that familiar with Long Island and what locations were best, but it was in an area that was more affordable and convenient to the highways for Jake to travel out east for work. One of the biggest things I hated about the area was that all three kids would go to three different schools. In Maine, they all went to one elementary school and one high school. In the school district we were in, the elementary school was split, one school for kindergarten through 2nd grade, and another school for 3rd grade through 5th grade. Then a separate middle school, and a separate high school. Shane was going into first grade and Marie would be in fourth grade in the upper elementary school. I thought that was crazy, but I guess because of all the students they had, they needed to break up the grades like that. I had lived on Long Island when I was in eleventh and twelfth grade, and I had moved from a class of thirty students in Upstate, NY to a graduating class of six hundred fifty students. That was a culture shock for me. I felt terrible for Claire who was going into 11th grade, but I knew there was nothing I could do about it. It might not be easy to make new friends, but I was glad that she at least had family down here. I just hoped that in time they would be glad that we moved.

We were getting settled into the routine of this new area and home. I had started a job at a deli nearby owned by my brother, and Jake seemed happy with the work he was doing and the money he was being paid. Claire was also working at the deli and school would begin soon. Claire had met a boy at the deli that she liked, and he would also go to the same high school. It was going to make it much more bearable for her to start a new school. He was going to be a senior and even though she wouldn't see him much during the day, just being able to go with him in the morning and come home together in the afternoon made a big difference. They also saw a lot of each other at work. I know this took some stress and worry off my shoulders because he was very kind to Claire, and she was happier.

It didn't take long before Jake started to sour on his new employment. Once again, he would come home from work complaining about the jobs and about something someone said or did. Jake was never happy working for somebody else, and here he was, once again, working for someone else. In Maine he was on his own, building his own homes, and working as a self-employed carpenter on other jobs. Jake couldn't stand anyone telling him what to do. He thought he could just do what he wanted, even if his boss had something else in mind. I could not understand why he thought he should make all the decisions when it wasn't his company. What made things even worse was that Jake always believed he was right, no one else was going to change that fact. It was the start of bad times ahead for all of us.

School began, and it seemed to go okay. The kids were getting used to the routine of three different schools and two different bus stops. However, I noticed that Shane wasn't acting like his normal, happy self. He had such an adorable face and a smile that just warmed your heart. He was such a loving child, always having fun, playing with his toys. I had hoped he would make lots of friends at school, but it turned out that he was having trouble. I overheard him saying to himself,

"You're stupid, you're dumb."

"What is wrong, honey?" I asked him.

"Nothing," he replied.

"Are you sure?" I asked.

"Mommy, I'm fine," he replied.

I didn't want to make a bigger deal out of it than it was, but I just kept my eyes and ears open because he just seemed different. I knew the move was a big change, but this felt worrisome.

I started getting more concerned about Shane. He just seemed so sad, and I couldn't pinpoint anything going on at home than the usual from his father, nothing to make such a difference in his personality. I mentioned it to Jake, but he just brushed it off. He never worried about anything going on with the kids unless it was something he didn't want them to do. One day after I came home from work, I was heading to Shane's room to check on him, and I overheard him saying to himself, "I'm stupid, I'm an idiot." It broke my heart hearing him saying this to himself. As I peeked into his room, he was standing with his back towards me, not yet knowing I was there, just uttering those words over and over, pacing back and forth with his head down, his little hands clenched in fists hitting himself on his legs. I had never seen him like this before. As I called out to him, he looked up at me with such a surprised and sad look on his face. I walked over to his bed and asked him to sit down with me. I pleaded with him to tell me what was going on. I told him, "No matter what you tell me I will not get upset or mad, just please tell me what is wrong." Shane broke down and told me he was being picked on by some boys on the school bus. They had been hitting him.

"What does the bus driver say?" I asked him.

"The bus driver doesn't even notice," Shane responded.

It was so disheartening hearing this. I didn't know what I should do except call the school to let them know and see what they could do about it. I didn't want to make the situation worse, but the school needed to know that this was happening. Shane seemed to feel better knowing that I was going to call the school. I'm sure he hoped I could stop this from happening, and I was hoping this would take care of it too. For the time being, I just kept it between the two of us until I could talk to the school.

The next morning, I called the school asking to talk to the principal. I was told that the situation on the bus would be checked on. I prayed the school administrators could sort this out and everything would get better for Shane. Unfortunately, nothing seemed to change, because a couple of days later Shane came home very sad and upset from school. I needed to talk to Jake about it because I didn't know what else to do. When Jake got home, after he entered the kitchen and opened his first beer, I told him what was going on at school with Shane. I told him I had already reported it to the school, but obviously nothing was being done about it. Like always, Jake didn't care what I was saying. He just turned away, as if annoyed, and started yelling for Shane to come into the kitchen. Jake was sitting at the table when Shane came into the room. Jake confronted Shane demanding to know about what was going on at school. As soon as Shane attempted to tell Jake that kids were picking on him, Jake yells at him, "You need to hit them back, you need to hit them harder than they hit you!"

Shane was only six years old, a very sweet and kind child. I understand no one wants to see their child bullied by another, but how is violence against violence going to help? The school handbook stated that any kind of violence was against school policy, and Shane could get in serious trouble. Telling a child to hurt another child is not the answer. But Jake wasn't done. I could see the anger building up in Jake. His face would always get red and, with his voice raising, his eyes got scary looking. He sat Shane down and started yelling, "You are to fight back. You don't let them bully you. You need to hit them so hard you make them bleed. I don't even want to hear that someone hit you and you didn't hit them back." Shane nor I could even get a word in, Jake was just going on and on. This was the advice that Jake had for his little son. A first grader. Violence. Shane began shaking, not daring to say anything back to his father. He was crying, and I knew he had to be frightened at the thought of having to hit another child. I don't think Shane understood why his father couldn't just get them to stop. Believe me, I understood Jake's frustration about not wanting someone to hit and pick on your child and that something had to be done about it, but this was not the answer. I argued with Jake and told Shane he does not have to hit anyone. I promised Shane that if it happened again, I would call the school again. Unfortunately, it did continue. When I called the school again, I was told, "There is nothing we can do about it unless someone sees it happening."

I set up a meeting with Shane's teacher, hoping she might give me some insight into what might be happening in school and on the bus. She told me that Shane was a very sweet sensitive boy and that he clung to her like he was not getting enough attention at home. I knew Jake didn't have any interest in spending time with Shane and, when he did, it was mostly negative attention. I believed that his sisters and I spent time with Shane, but maybe not enough time. I believed Shane was clinging to his teacher because he was afraid of being at school with kids picking on him and nothing being done to stop it. I must admit, I felt hurt by his teacher's comments, but it was the truth, Shane needed more from us.

Jake had wanted a son so badly, and yet when it came to spending time with Shane, he never did. All Jake did was work, come home, watch TV and drink his beer. The most attention he would give the kids was to ask them about school and if they got their schoolwork done

Anytime Jake asked about school, the kids would just say "It's fine," and that would be the end of the conversation. They didn't dare say anything else, especially negative, because they didn't know how Jake would react to it and didn't want to find out. Shane kept trying to pretend that everything was going better at school, but you could tell it was not. We all preferred that Jake would just drink his beer and stay clear of us.

Shane, being the sensitive boy he was, couldn't hide the fact that things were not getting any better. It turned out that not only was Shane being picked on when on the bus, but now they were hitting him in the locker room where no one could see them. They made sure no teachers were around so they couldn't get caught. It's pretty scary that at such a young age these kids were smart enough to do this and get away with it. It's pretty obvious that they had been doing this for some time now and I'm sure not just with Shane. Every day, when Jake got home from work, he would grill Shane and would want to know what Shane did about it. It had become a ritual.

This brings us back to that fretful night and those words echoing in my brain, "If you don't fucking kill him, then I will fucking kill you."

How did I not grab the kids and run? Shane needed help, not the horrible words and mental abuse that Jake was inflicting on him. This, though, was much more than that. Jake would interrogate Shane every day after school but knew the answers, which enraged Jake even more. The kids bullied him, and ganged up on him, and he was powerless to stop it. So, what was Jake's solution? Kill them. He screamed at Shane to murder another boy, or he would come home and face what a 6-year-old could only know, at the time, meant certain death, because here his father was promising to kill him if he did not follow through with it. I will never understand how Jake could be so cruel and how I could allow this abuse to go on. What did I do after hearing this? Nothing. I said and did nothing. We were living on Long Island now with my family all around me, and I still did nothing and said nothing to any of them about what Jake had just said to our son. I blocked it out and never even spoke of it again with Jake, as if it had never happened. This was what I did after every hurtful thing Jake said or did. What the hell was wrong with me? If only I weren't so intimidated and afraid to speak up, afraid of where the kids and I would go and how we would survive. If I had spoken up, my family would have helped me leave Jake, but I will never know, because I did nothing. No matter how hard it might have been to make it on my own, it would have been better than staying and putting the kids through all the years of abuse ahead of them. Shameful!

I remember each evening, sitting in the living room with the usual pit in my stomach, just knowing that Jake would be home soon. Would he be in a good mood, foul mood, or just downright angry? We never knew until he came through that door and started talking to me. I would always walk on eggshells, waiting for what he might say or how the evening would go. I always dreaded him coming home. Of course, Jake always had to come home carrying that six-pack or twelve-pack of beer with him. Oh, how I hate Budweiser. I guess it depended on his day how much beer Jake would need to get through the night. I wish I could say his anger and abuse was all because of the beer, but it wasn't, it just made it worse.

Getting back to that evening, Jake came in the door with his usual "Hi." Not a happy "Hi", just a gruff greeting and then straight to the kitchen to put the beer away. I had come to hate the sound of a beer can popping open. I knew what came next. Who would he complain about today? Who looked at him wrong, who insulted him by making a joke. Jake could dish it out, but he could never take it. Which one of us would he take it out on? Probably all of us. This evening it was Shane, who would soon become Jake's daily target of choice.

I didn't realize that Shane had gone into the kitchen before me. Of course, the first thing Jake wanted to talk about was whether he stood up for himself today and hit back. Shane did not give him the answer he wanted, and that's when I heard the horrible yelling start. As I headed towards the kitchen, I heard Jake scream at Shane, "If you don't fucking kill him, then I will fucking kill you!!" What??? Was I hearing things, did he just say that to our six-year-old son?

I am trying to calm Shane down, I can feel him shaking with fear, crying and so afraid, not from the bullies at school, but from his father. Jake's face is beat red with anger, and he is out of control. I started screaming at Jake, I couldn't believe what he had just said. I felt like I was in shock, like this really didn't just happen, but it did. I quickly put my arms around Shane and pulled him out of the kitchen and we went into his room so I could try to calm him down and talk to him about what his father had just said. I tried to explain that his father didn't mean what he just said. I tried to reassure him that everything would be okay, but would it be? I told Shane that "Tomorrow I will call the school and put a stop to this bullying." I was desperate, because I knew the school would be no help, plus now it was worse at home than it was at school. Jake had warned Shane, "I don't care if you get in trouble, you better kill this fucking kid. I'll handle it if you get in trouble." It was so traumatizing and hard to imagine that Jake could be this cruel to his youngest child. If I hadn't heard the words myself, I never would have believed Jake would stoop that low. The rest of the evening was a blur. I don't remember if Jake and I continued fighting over it. I'm not sure if the girls heard any of it, or if I blocked it out almost as quick as it happened. It was frightening to know Jake could be that angry, that cruel to his own son and at only six years of age, never mind any age. What would happen next?

The next day, while I was at work, I received a phone call from Shane's school. I was concerned and wondered why the school was calling, thinking something else had happened, but I wasn't prepared for why they were actually calling. Nervously picking up the phone to say hello, I hear a woman on the other end say to me "We have Shane here in the office, and we're not allowing him to go home on the bus. You need to come pick him up because an incident has happened at school." She refused to discuss it over the phone. I can remember feeling very nervous, sick to my stomach, wondering what had happened now. I just knew I needed to get there as soon as possible and prayed that it wouldn't be anything too bad.

As I entered the school and announced who I was, they took me into the principal's office. I noticed Shane was not in the room. Shane's teacher and the principal greeted me, asking me to sit down. His teacher then said, "Shane told another child in his classroom today that he was going to kill himself and use his Daddy's gun, which is behind the door in your bedroom." I was stunned! I never even thought it could be possible that a child Shane's age would feel so low that he would even think of wanting to kill himself. But now decades later, as I write this, I realize why wouldn't Shane feel that way, after his dad just told Shane he would kill him if he didn't kill another child. What the Hell!! Of course, that's going to screw someone's mind up. In addition to being sweet and kind, Shane was very intelligent. He had figured out a way to make it all stop.

I felt like such a failed parent. How could I have let this happen? I allowed this man to make Shane feel like he had no other choice but to kill himself so he wouldn't be forced to kill someone else. I can't even imagine what Shane was going through. Does a six-year-old even know what it means to kill someone, or even what it means to kill himself? How the hell did I let it get to this point? I cannot change anything now, but it's hard to face what a coward I was. I let down all my children and allowed things like this to happen, not realizing the damage I was doing to them. I thought I was doing what I needed to do to protect us all, but I was wrong, very wrong.

The principal told me they had called social services and that the only way I could bring Shane home was if I agreed to let social services come to our home. They needed to see where Shane lived, his bedroom, the environment, and talk to both of his parents. Of course, I said yes. What choice did I have? I don't know what frightened me more, Shane being scarred by what happened, or what Jake was going to do or say when he was told about this. I feared for all of us!

As soon as I got home, I called Jake. I could feel this sick, overwhelming feeling creeping up in my stomach and then my chest. I could feel my body trembling, my hands shaking as I picked up the phone to call him. When he answered the phone, I remember myself saying,

"Jake, you need to come home, now!
Something happened at school, and we have people
from social services heading to our house."
I can't remember everything he said, but I know he asked,
"What the hell happened?" I told him,
"Shane said he wanted to kill himself and that he was
going to use your gun."
I remember Jake getting furious and hanging up.

Jake, of course, arrived home in a fury. As soon as he came through the door and up the stairs, he yelled, "What the hell is going on?" I couldn't believe he was going to get defensive and act rude to the woman from social services before even entering the living room where they were waiting for him. There were two of them, I don't recall their names. One seemed more in charge of the situation than the other, because she did most of the talking.

She asked Jake to sit down and sternly responded saying
  "Your son, Shane, talked about killing himself and
    had a plan of using your gun to do it, and said he
    knows where your gun is."
She was not intimidated at all by Jake's attitude. I am sure they dealt with people like him before. I was glad to see that. Jake responded,
  "I don't know why he would say that."
I was no better, because I said nothing. I just sat there on the couch, next to Jake, Shane was sitting on the floor across from us closer to where the woman was sitting. I was so nervous, worrying about what to say and what not to say. It was a fine line that could either keep Shane with us or make them take him away from us. I couldn't tell them what had happened last night or what life was like here at home because I could lose my

son. I would rather die than let them take him away from us. I guess I was being selfish and only thinking about myself, but at the time I thought I was doing the right thing for him. I was nervous sitting next to Jake, waiting for him to just explode, making things worse. I believed that although home was not good, it would devastate Shane if they took him away from his sisters and me, not being able to see us or talk to us daily. A six-year-old boy being taken away from his mother, I couldn't bear it. It was so frightening to even think about.

They continued talking to us about sending Shane to a children's psychiatric facility in Amityville, where we wouldn't see him for a month or more. I could not imagine that. I started crying, disagreeing with them because I knew it would devastate Shane if they took him away from us. I begged,

"Isn't there something else we can do, please?!"

"Let me make a phone call." She said.

I sat there praying to God that they would not take him. You could tell how furious Jake was, but he wasn't saying much at this point. He most likely didn't want to say something that could be used against him or make him look bad. Maybe he believed Shane would say something about what had happened last night. I don't know, but I was glad he kept quiet at this point. Of course, I knew the anger was building up inside him and he was going to explode once they left, but I would deal with that later. All that mattered was what was happening now. When she hung up the phone, she told us that if we brought Shane right away to Bellevue Hospital for an evaluation to make sure he wasn't a danger to himself, they would let him stay with us if the hospital believed he wasn't in danger. If the hospital staff believed he was a danger to himself, they would admit him immediately following that visit. We agreed. We had to agree if we wanted any chance of keeping him with us. Of course, my reason for wanting to keep him with us differed from his father's. He was more worried about how it would affect him and what Shane might say. I'm sure Shane would have been better off in the long run, but we'll never know. I didn't allow it to happen.

After they left, we headed to Bellevue. I can't recall if we talked on the car ride or not, but most likely Jake was watching what he said, so Shane didn't repeat it to the doctor. I can remember being in the hospital room. It was dingy with crème-colored walls. I remember the hospital bed having dried blood on the bed frame below the mattress. It was gross, but I knew I had bigger issues to deal with, so I just ignored it. I just wanted to get in and out of there as soon as possible and take my son home. I remember the doctor coming in. I can't remember if he talked to Shane alone before he talked to us, but I know Shane was acting like his old cheerful happy self. Shane was talking with the doctor, smiling, acting like nothing was wrong with him or his home life. He didn't give the doctor any reason for concern, and so the doctor agreed that Shane didn't need to go into the hospital, he needed outpatient therapy to address any issues. They gave us a referral to a children's therapist and the next day I set up Shane's first appointment.

For Shane, therapy was going great. He seemed happy with his therapist, and it was great seeing glimpses of my sweet, loving boy again without all the fear he was carrying. Jake was on his best behavior because he didn't want Shane to mention anything bad about him during therapy and didn't want social services involved in his life. When Jake and I were alone, he argued with me about it because he didn't believe in therapy, but I didn't care. I was just glad that Shane was getting the help he needed, that was all that mattered.

It was much more peaceful at home now. Not perfect, but Shane was not getting bullied at home by his father, and his therapist was helping him deal with the kids at school and teaching him that it was okay not to fight back, that there was nothing wrong with him, and that it was the kids bullying him that have the issues. Shane would tell me what the therapist would tell him, and I was ecstatic to see how much it was helping him and how much he enjoyed being able to talk to someone. His therapist made him feel at ease and safe. Shane needed that, needed someone who would listen to him about anything he needed to talk about, and have calm conversations with him that were not about hurting other children.

Marie was not having any issues at school and was doing well. Marie and Shane made good friends with the neighbors' kids and were having fun hanging out with them after school and on weekends. They seemed to get along well, and I was glad to see that. Claire was busy between school, working part-time, and spending time with her new boyfriend. I was glad she didn't get depressed like I did when I moved to Long Island in my junior year from a small rural town with a large class of students who already had their clicks, making it hard to make new friends.

It was nice that my job was right down the road, and I didn't have to worry about being stuck in traffic for hours trying to get home. I had plenty of time to see the kids and make dinner before Jake got home. My hours worked well with the kid's school schedule, and for a while, things were looking up. Unfortunately, that was short-lived. After the second year of renting this house, the landlord was raising our rent and Jake was not about to pay more than he already did. Once again, he wanted to move. The kids would have to start over again in another school, losing the friends they had just made. I would also have to find another job because this one would be too far to travel to and still work around the kid's school schedule.

Jake knew what to say to make it sound exciting. He said he would rather pay a mortgage than pay rent to somebody, so he decided we would look into buying a house on Long Island. All I ever wanted was a house, a home we could call our own and finally stay in one place. I thought maybe he had found his niche working on the houses out East, maybe things would get better. I always tried to have hope. We decided we would look for a home closer to his work in areas where the houses were cheaper.

Right off the bat, Jake started complaining about the house prices. You would think he didn't already know that Long Island was expensive, that he was going to pay more than he would if we still lived in Maine. In some areas prices were still reasonable for Long Island, and we could have bought a house that would have gone up in value quickly if he just wasn't so stubborn. Every house we looked at Jake had something negative to say.

"I can build us a house much cheaper, there's no way I'm paying these prices." If he was going to build us a house, he would have done it already. Every house we looked at was never good enough, and not built to his liking. As a carpenter, none of them were going to measure up to what he thought was right. These homes were old, they were going to have flaws and issues, but he knew that, and it was just an excuse to reject them all. If he wanted to work on Long Island, he would have to pay Long Island prices and no amount of complaining was going to change that fact.

Someone had mentioned to us that the Rocky Point area was still affordable because the houses were small, more like cottages, and the area had not grown yet. We had heard that it was a very nice, safe area to live and raise your kids. I was so excited at the thought of finding a home there, that we might actually do it. I think I was more excited because I knew Jake would never build us a "forever" home, it was always empty promises. Maybe this time, since he wanted to pay a mortgage rather than rent, we could be settled once and for all, especially in a location where he could make good money.

We found a small red brick home in Rocky Point that we both liked and thought was cute. From the outside you could tell it was small, but it had potential.

It was a red brick ranch-style home with a small backyard. Nothing fancy, but you could make it even nicer by adding a front porch or nice entryway. As you entered the front door, you were in the living room area. It was not huge, but it was big enough for us. Straight ahead from the living area was the kitchen which looked so unique. As you entered the kitchen, you felt like you were in a time warp. They designed it like the 50s or 60s with old-fashioned, light blue appliances you never saw anymore, but they were in excellent shape, and I loved the look. I would just keep it the way it was, and Jake would like that he wouldn't have to spend money fixing it up, at this point anyway, until he needed to. I believe it had one full bathroom and three small bedrooms. It was plenty of room for us, seeing that Claire was graduating and not planning on moving out East with us and Tara was already living on her own. In the future, Jake could add a second floor if he wanted to or if we thought we needed the extra space.

It was selling for $220,000, which was a great price for a house on Long Island at that time. Even though the house was small, all homes were so expensive and before long Rocky Point was going to be an expensive area too. We could build equity in this home. I was so excited, and Jake knew how much I wanted this house, and he knew it was the cheapest he was going to find here, which mattered most, so he agreed to make an offer. Jake made an offer of $200,000. I thought, "Wow, this is really going to happen."

The owners countered with an offer of $204,000. I was so excited. I believed that was a great counteroffer, considering that Jake had asked $20,000 under the asking price, but he didn't agree. Jake refused the offer and said he would not pay a penny more than what he offered. It was then that I realized he had no intention of ever buying this house. That is why he bid so low. Even if they had agreed to the $200,000, he would have found another reason to back out. This was all a ruse, pretending to do something he never intended to do. What a fool I was to have thought this was going to happen and once again have the hope of a home taken away. Clearly upset by his decision, he became furious that I was so disappointed and disheartened. His split personality came through with a vengeance. He went from wanting this house to being irate that it upset me because he wouldn't buy this house, and he just became unglued.

We were heading home on the Long Island Expressway; Jake was screaming and yelling about how ridiculous the price was and how he refused to buy a house on Long Island when he could build one for half the price. He was out of control with his screaming, and the kids and I were crying and scared to death at this point. Jake was driving erratically on the highway, and I honestly thought he would kill us all in an accident. By the time we got home, I could feel myself shaking, distraught with fear after witnessing the irrational screaming and erratic driving that I had never seen so out of control before. As if a switch flipped as we entered the driveway, his rage ended. The sudden change didn't even seem to faze him. He just walked into the house like nothing had happened.

I was still shaking, and I'm sure the kids were too. I went into the house, went straight into our bedrooms and packed some clothes for the kids and myself. I walked out to the living room and told Jake, "I am leaving, we are not living like this anymore." I took my kids, and we headed to my sister's house. She lived out East in Mattituck. I didn't know what I was doing, but I knew something had to change. He endangered the kids' lives, and that was not okay.

I appreciated my sister taking us in on such brief notice. It would not be easy, all of us in her house, but we were going to make it work for the time being until I could figure out what to do. The kids would have to start again in a new school, but they didn't seem too upset about it. It turned out they liked this school, and Shane had no issues with kids being mean or trying to bully him. Shane continued his therapy appointments, which helped with the transition. I knew it was best for him to continue going and I could already see this therapist made a big difference in him, so I didn't want him to have to start again with a new one. Meanwhile, Jake rented an apartment out East in Manorville. Not that far from us, which made it easy for him to visit the kids and for me to bring the kids to him. I preferred bringing them to him, only because he made it obvious that he was not a fan of my sister and gave her an attitude every time he came to see the kids. She gave it right back, and he did not like that. No woman was going to talk back to him and, as far as he was concerned, she was to blame. He believed she talked me into leaving him, and that I wouldn't have thought of this on my own. I suppose he believed I would have come right back home, but she must have talked me out of it. He always had to blame somebody else. Nothing was ever his fault.

I hated going to Jake's place to drop the kids off because he would always try to sweet-talk me with promises he would make. He acted like he was going to change, begging me to come back to him. And of course, he would always do this in front of the children and then the kids would want to go back because they would feel bad. Even though Shane was the brunt of Jake's anger, he was a young boy who wanted his father's love and approval more than anything. I hated myself for still loving Jake. What a fool to love someone who was so wrong for you and who would put us through this.

It only took a few months before I gave in and went back to him. He promised if we moved to Upstate New York, he would buy us a house. He knew how much I loved it up there and would love to live there. It didn't take too much convincing. I hoped the kids would love it just as much as I did. I hated that they would have to change schools once again, but they were eager to have bedrooms of their own and they missed their father. It was also obvious that it would never work staying at my sister's house. We couldn't stay there forever. It was not big enough for all of us, and I knew it was a hardship for her and her family too. I also felt it was hard on Shane being the only boy in a household with five females. He always seemed to be the one who was doing something wrong. I just didn't know how I was ever going to afford a place of our own on Long Island, so what choice did I really have? I felt like I had no other choice but to try again, and hoped that this time it would be different. Part of me thought that perhaps Jake would take me seriously now. I left him once; I could do it again if he didn't change. Also, I was thinking it would be like rural Maine, so maybe Jake would be happier up there. He was not a city boy, and Long Island was a city to him. I'm sure he only cared about getting us away from my family, which was the only thing I hated about moving away from Long Island.

The kids seemed happy to be moving to the country. They would miss their cousins, but they didn't like Long Island. I hated leaving my mother and my siblings, but the memories from my childhood were so strong and were some of the best for me. It was like going home. The hardest part was leaving Claire. She would not be moving with us. She had moved into an apartment with her boyfriend to live her own life, and who could blame her? I wouldn't want to come with us either if I were her. Thank heaven she visited often, though. It was hard enough that Tara was all the way in Vermont at that point. She had moved from Maine to Vermont, and she loved it there. She deserved everything she wanted out of life. I so wanted her to be happy.

I wasn't concerned about the move this time because I knew the area. At first, Jake tried to get me to move to a different area upstate, not where I grew up, but I stood my ground and said the only way I would move upstate with him was if we were near where I grew up. I needed to feel safe and know my way around the area, seeing that I didn't have any family living up there. That was the only way I was going to feel comfortable leaving everyone, plus I knew my family liked to visit that area, so I knew I would get to see them as often as they could get away. Jake didn't seem concerned about whether he would find work, so I didn't worry either. I knew we would find something, and it was a more affordable place to live, and beautiful too.

My sister helped me look for houses on the real estate sites, and we drove Upstate to check some of them out. Jake was busy with work, and I was just as pleased to get to do this without him. He wasn't patient at all with us finding a house. He made it quite stressful, Saying "If you don't find something soon, we'll just buy a piece of land and I'll put a trailer on it until I can build us a house." Just hearing those words made my skin crawl. I knew he would never build us a house, not one he would keep for us. If that was true, he would have already done it. I felt like I had to hurry and find something before he changed his mind. After a few disappointments, we found a house we both liked, and the price and location seemed perfect.

It was a large, beautiful old home in the town of Worcester. It was close to where I grew up, just the next town over. I couldn't have been any happier with the location. The house was white, Victorian style, with a large wrap-around porch. I couldn't believe it was going to be mine, finally a home for my kids, our family. It was old and needed a lot of work, but its bones were strong and beautiful. Jake had all these ideas of how he was going to make it so nice for us and seemed excited about this house. It was nice to have a large yard again with woods behind it for the kids to explore like I did when I was a child.

It was a new beginning.

Chapter

5

Praying For A Change

Jake decided we would drive up to Worcester on Thanksgiving Day, most likely because there would be less traffic. But I'm sure he was also happy he wouldn't have to spend the holiday with my family. The weather was not cooperating, and we were having a snowstorm. Jake wasn't about to let bad weather stop us from leaving. I prayed the roads were not icy, and mostly it was a pleasant drive. We were just excited to move to our new home and hopefully start a new, happier beginning. All these years later, I was still hopeful. I see now that was idiotic of me.

The kids were excited to have a new home where they each had their own space once again. I'm sure they were nervous about starting another new school, but they didn't complain about it. They seemed thrilled. When we arrived in the area, we stopped at a diner to have our Thanksgiving dinner, which was not Turkey with the trimmings, but we were glad to have the drive over with. The kids were anxious to see the house, as they had only seen pictures.

Heading out of the town of Worcester, we pulled up to our new house. It was dark and snowing outside, but I can still see our big white house in the distance with the streetlights shining. I could not believe it was ours, it looked so pretty with its wrap-around front porch and green shutters. As we drove up the slightly steep driveway, a large barn was on the right. It needed some work but would make a great workshop for Jake. The house was up on a hill, and from our large side yard you could see down into the town and the many side roads that led to it.

On the side of the house was an entrance that led to an attached mudroom where we could leave our wet boots and coats. From there, a door led into the large kitchen. The floor of the kitchen was covered in purple outdoor carpeting that we found out later was glued onto the cement slab. It was hideous, but nothing that couldn't be replaced. To the right was a narrow staircase that led to the master bedroom. Straight ahead, in the right back corner of the kitchen, was an enormous stone fireplace with a stone shelf below it for holding hot pots and pans. They used this fireplace for cooking many years ago. I thought it was unusual to not be in the living room, but I liked it anyway and enjoyed sitting in front of it from time to time. Across from the fireplace were the kitchen cabinets, sink, and stove area. The stove was old and unique, but we liked it and would use it for now. The cabinets were nothing fancy but gave us a lot of space. At some point, the entire kitchen would have to be updated. For now, it was usable. To the left of the door was the refrigerator and a large area for a kitchen table and chairs. There was a lot of potential with this kitchen, and it could be as beautiful as we chose to make it.

To the left of the cabinets was the entrance into the dining room. As you entered the dining room, on your left was a nice built-in hutch and to the right was a curved wall facing the yard with three large windows. Two more windows looked out onto the wrap-around porch. There was hardwood flooring and wainscoting on all the walls. There was dentil crown molding trim all around the ceiling, which looked wonderful. It was beautiful.

Through the dining room you entered the extremely large living area. It has the same dentil crown molding all around it and hardwood floors that were in fairly decent shape. In the middle of the living area, on your right, was the large wooden front door that led to the large, covered wrap-around porch. On the left side of the living area was another staircase leading up to the bedrooms. We could use part of this room as the living room and the other half as an office or library area. Next to the staircase was a small half bathroom, nothing fancy but great to have. At the top of the stairs was our bedroom on the right and straight ahead was Shane's bedroom. Around the banister was a spare bedroom, and further down was Marie's bedroom and a full bathroom.

Our bedroom was large with a nice-sized picture window letting in a lot of sunlight. They had painted it an ugly blue color which we would have to change. Along one wall was a large closet, and on the opposite side of the room was the narrow staircase that led to the kitchen. We also had a half-bathroom.

Shane's bedroom was a good size. His room had some old-fashioned wallpaper, but he didn't care. He was just so happy to have his own room. He had one small window, a small closet, a built-in bookcase, and plenty of room for his bed and toys. Marie's room was also a nice size with two large windows. It also had old-fashioned wallpaper. She decorated her room very cute and loved that she had her own space away from us. Jake allowed her to hang up some posters, and we hung nice curtains and shelves. The hallway outside the bedrooms had hideous wallpaper, so I painted over it for the time being just to brighten it up a little as a temporary fix for now. I planned to eventually remove the old wallpaper and update these rooms, but for now they were very livable.

Jake would talk about all the things he was going to fix on the house and how great it was going to look. I was very excited at the thought. He talked about putting copper on the roof of the front porch to dress it up. He would need to redo the kitchen first, starting with insulation, which it didn't have. I believe the kitchen and our bedroom were the original structure, and then someone added on the rest of the house years later and never got around to fixing up the kitchen. All I knew was, this house could be beautiful once Jake went to work on it.

Everything was going pretty well. I was just a little worried because I wasn't finding a job as easily as Jake had. He lined up some carpentry work and worked for himself, which he always preferred to do. It was a lot cheaper to live up here, and our mortgage was half of what our rent on Long Island was. The kids started school after Thanksgiving vacation, and it seemed to go well. I know it was hard starting again, but all I could do was hope they liked it here and made a lot of friends. They had already made friends with the neighbor's girls that lived down the hill below us. One of their girls was about Shane's age and a tomboy, so they liked the same things and got along well.

It didn't take long before we settled in and the excitement of our new beginning was wearing off. Jake was starting to act his usual self, complaining about the kids, his work, and now even talking about selling the house once he fixes it up. He would talk about all the things he could do to make it so nice, but not for us. Only to sell it and make money from it. I could almost see the dollar signs ($$) in his eyes. He just could not be satisfied with what he had. He never cared about making us feel secure and finally grounded. It was the same old thing, just a different place to do it. And here I was again, questioning why I thought it would be any better. I should have realized you cannot change someone's personality, and his was a very negative one. He only seemed happy when he was complaining or upsetting one of us. One time after we had a fight, he saw how upset I was, and told me, "I enjoy fighting", and he meant it. He would have a grin on his face so I could see the pleasure it gave him seeing me upset.

We could truly have had a great, fulfilling life. We had a beautiful home in a very nice town, we had stability because it wasn't terribly expensive to live there. Sadly, none of that mattered to him. I couldn't understand why he preferred to be so uncaring and angry all the time about everything. When was I going to take the blinders off and realize once and for all that we would never have a home, and we would never be a happy family? I hate how foolish and dumb I was for all those years, believing it would get better with time. How many more years was I going to keep imagining it would get better? I just kept letting this man get my hopes up, just so he could crush them once again. I don't even know how I was still mentally and emotionally standing at this point.

Before long, Shane was once again having trouble at school with some kids. This time it was different. With Shane being older, he was now fighting back and getting detention. He was trying to prove something to his father. His father had said to him, "I don't care if you're getting detention, just as long as you're hitting back." Now Shane was not only hitting back, he was starting the fights. It was like a vicious cycle; he did not want to be bullied, so he became the bully. Sadly, he was doing this to please his father, although it didn't matter. Shane would come home from school and tell how he fought back, and his father would call him a liar and choose not to believe him. It didn't matter what Shane did to please his father; it would never be enough, and Shane was being destroyed by it.

As time went on, our lives just seemed to get worse. The fighting was always out of control and his drinking was definitely much worse. Jake was never going to be happy and he was damn well making sure that none of us were going to be happy either. At this point the kids and I were also uncomfortable because once again, Jake had his rifle loaded and visible so we knew it was there. It was his way of keeping the fear in me, and it worked. I needed to talk to him about these things. One night after work after he started his usual drinking of a six-pack or more, I tried talking to him about stopping the drinking, which of course then turned into an argument. In the heat of the moment, I asked him,

"Are you saying that drinking beer is

more important than us?" and he responded,

"Yes! At this time, it is. Besides, I don't

believe I drink too much".

I can't say it surprised me, but I still didn't expect him to say that. I told him how I felt about the gun and all he said about that was "Don't worry, I'm not going to shoot you". Nothing I said meant anything to him. He was content with his miserable life as long as he had us to take it out on and to be just as miserable. I just cried and once again told the kids to pack up a bag and we left our home and drove back to Long Island. We went to my sister's house again, this time I thought it was for good.

I just couldn't take it anymore knowing that the kids and I deserved so much better. Shane was now 11 years old and Marie was 14. How many times could I keep going back and forth? It's just so hard when you have no money in the bank, and your sister already has a full house. Here I go again, needing a place to stay. I accepted her gracious offer, even though I knew she didn't have enough room. She never once made me feel like she didn't want us there. I truly appreciated her welcoming us back into her house, and I know she just wanted what was best for me and the kids.

Jake was constantly calling and talking to Shane. He would tell Shane to beg me to let him stay with his dad. Shane was a child who desperately wanted his father in his life, seeking his love and acceptance. Jake had Shane convinced that he would be different.

Then Jake started saying that he would come get Shane and bring him back home with him. I could not let that happen, I would never allow Shane to live alone with Jake with his drinking and his temper. The idea was terrifying. I felt like I had no choice but to go back. I had this 11-year-old child begging me to go home so he could see his father. I couldn't blame Shane and I couldn't fight it. Jake knew exactly how to control the situation. The one difference this time was that I knew I no longer loved this man, I just hated him. I had loved him for so many years but now that was gone. He had finally killed it. I decided I would go back there, but only until Shane was old enough to tell a judge he didn't want overnight visits with him. I knew I needed to protect him. Obviously, I never did protect him. I was only kidding myself. I allowed all this verbal and emotional abuse to continue, not realizing the damage it did could be worse than physical abuse. I was just so afraid because I believed it was only a matter of time before Jake would become extremely physical with Shane. Already Jake would grab Shane's arm in anger, not letting him go until he was done yelling at him. At other times, Jake would pretend he wanted to rough house with Shane, just playing, but Shane always ended up hurt and crying. Jake would just laugh and say, "I told him to stop, but he wouldn't listen so I had to hurt him to get him to stop." His goal was to hurt him and then act like it was Shane's fault.

Marie didn't seem to be the brunt of most of Jake's temper. Even if Marie did something wrong that pissed him off, he would try and somehow turn it on Shane and yell at him. Marie was so upset every time he would yell at Shane and blame him for everything. She would cry to me about how bad she felt and the guilt she felt over her dad treating her better than Shane. She could not understand it. Of course, how could she? It was irrational behavior with no justification.

Once I returned to Worcester, I found a job at a local hospital and worked 12-hour shifts 3-4 days a week. I had to leave before the kids got on the bus in the morning and didn't get home until close to 8 p.m. At least it wasn't the graveyard shift and five days a week like my past job. Marie hated the fact that her father would get home before me on the days I worked, but there was nothing I could do to change that. This was the best job for me. It allowed me to be home with the kids more days and it had much-needed health benefits.

When I would come home from work, I would hear from the kids how the day had gone. There was always something bad they needed to tell me. It had to be very stressful for Marie being the older sister, not being able to protect Shane, knowing he was going to get in trouble for something, anything that would be an excuse to scream at him and possibly put his hands on him. Jake was getting rougher with Shane. Grabbing his arm roughly, shaking him in anger. Once, Jake started kicking Shane in the butt while he was down on the floor because he was mad about something. I had no way of knowing what was happening while I was at work, and I dreaded going home each day.

How frightening it must have been for Marie and Shane to never know if their dad's threats were going to happen. Jake would repeatedly say to Shane, "I'm going to beat the shit out of you," with his hands clenched and raised up like he's going to strike him. I felt that if he ever struck one of us like that, it would not end well. With his anger, I believed he would lose control until it was too late to stop.

Marie avoided being around her father as much as possible by staying in her bedroom. She would just say that she was working on schoolwork. Shane couldn't avoid seeing his father, even when in his bedroom. Jake would come looking for him just so he could yell at him for something. It didn't matter why he was mad. We were all becoming more frightened of Jake. He was drinking so much more, and his anger was intimidating and worrisome. One night my son said to me, "Mommy, I'm sorry I begged you to come back to Daddy. I was wrong, I don't want to be here anymore." My heart just sank. I explained to him that it wasn't his fault at all, it was my decision and my fault that we came back.

Tara knew that Marie and Shane were going through what she and Claire had gone through. She could not understand why I was allowing this to happen. Why was I staying with him? How could I explain it to her when I couldn't understand it myself? I felt like I had no choice. She begged me to let Shane and Marie live with her in Vermont if I was not willing to leave Jake. I was hurt and insulted that she would ask me this. How could she expect me to give them to her? I loved them and couldn't be without them. That's all I could think about. I would die inside without them. What would I have left to live for if I didn't have my children? I also knew that Jake would never allow that to happen. Looking back now, I know they would have been better off. I wish we all had left him and moved to Vermont with Tara. Of course, their father would have just come after us. I really couldn't see a way out.

I can remember the day I told Jake exactly what I thought of him and how I would leave him as soon as the kids were old enough to make their own decisions and could decide for themselves if they wanted to see him. I told him I'd leave as soon as Shane was old enough so that a judge would listen if Jake tried to fight for custody. I think in the back of my mind I was still listening to Tara's plea to stand up to him and get away before it was too late. We had another one of our usual fights over his treatment of Shane. I ran upstairs to my bedroom and Jake, of course, followed me so he could continue. Barely holding on to my sanity, crying and feeling depressed, I started yelling,

"As soon as Shane is 14, I'm taking the kids
away from here for good. I would rather be
dead then be here with you."

With a surprised look on his face, he has the nerve to say to me,

"I don't understand why you're so upset
all the time. You think it's that bad?"

I was stunned by his reaction. He seemed surprised that I thought It was that bad yet had no reaction to my saying I would rather be dead than be with him. Still, he won't let me leave. He wants us there because who else can he take his rage out on? I know he doesn't believe I will leave, anyway. I thought to myself that any normal man would have said, "Then just leave," but not Jake. As long as we're there for him to abuse, that's all he cares about. I kept thinking I needed to stay until Shane was 16, but I knew mentally I would not make it that long, I would take the chance that a judge might listen to a 14-year-old.

After this happened, I talked to a friend, and they offered me an anti-depressant to see if it would help me get through this time. They had switched to another medication and still had a lot left over. I remember after a few months of taking it, it seemed to help. I should have gone to a doctor, but I thought it couldn't hurt to try it first. The medicine helped me feel better, somehow less stressed and not worried about the future. I woke up one night in severe pain, needing to go to the emergency room, and ended up in surgery for a ruptured appendix. It turns out, my appendix ruptured one or two weeks prior, encapsulating in one area so it didn't cause me any serious complications. At the hospital, they asked me if I was taking any medications, but I didn't mention it because I felt guilty for taking it without a prescription. I decided to stop taking it until I saw a doctor to get my own prescription.

The next day, Jake came to the hospital with the kids, acting like the doting husband. I could tell the kids were glad to see me, but seemed very anxious. Right away Jake started complaining because he found out I had to stay another night and he would have to take care of his own kids. I don't remember everything he said, but I know I was crying and when he left the room briefly, the kids started begging me to come home, saying their father was being mean to them. What could I do? I hated knowing they were alone with him, but I had to be here, even if I didn't want to be. This was not fair. After Jake returned to the room, the nurse came in and he acted so sweet and concerned about me. He chatted with her about my treatment and, as she left the room, she turned to me and said, "How nice it is for you to have such a doting husband." Yuk!! It made me sick to hear this when right before she came in, he had me in tears, so angry that I had to stay another night. He didn't care that I just had surgery, he only cared about himself and that he had to take care of the kids. He would have to work his life around them for once. Our entire life always revolved around his needs and what he wanted.

Jake and I were lucky that I stopped taking the anti-depressant. It wasn't until the medicine was out of my system that I realized how it was affecting me. I must have been in some kind of mental euphoria. I am not sure how to explain it, but if I had not had the surgery and continued taking the antidepressant, I believe I would have most likely ended mine and Jake's life. I started remembering a plan I had formulated. In that state of mind, I had decided that the plan was the answer to all my problems. I'd decided that the kids would be better off if I killed Jake and then myself. Marie could live with my brother, his wife and family, and Shane could live with Tara in Vermont, who I thought would better understand what Shane needed. I knew I could never go to jail and needed to get this monster out of their lives. I was sure that the only way out was to end both of our lives. I remembered feeling better, like I had finally come up with the answer to all my problems. I had a plan and was going to do this. Going off the anti-depressant saved me. How horrified I was when I realized the fact that I was not in my right mind, and that this was a plan that might have happened. I can only believe that God helped me, knowing this was not something I would ever normally plan to do, and for that reason, I ended up needing surgery and stopping the medication. It is very scary to think that certain medications can alter your perception of reality. I kept this to myself until years later, when I told my family.

One evening, Jake received a phone call about his father who was very ill. He had a blood infection from a previous hip replacement surgery that didn't go well, causing him to have his leg amputated. If Jake wanted to see him, he should come now because they didn't know how much longer he would survive. His father lived in

Florida and was back at home. All of his siblings were coming there to see him, most likely, for the last time. It was the same week that the kids and I were going on my family's camping trip, but I knew we needed to skip this year and be with Jake, even though Marie and Shane had never met their grandfather before, as well as some of Jake's siblings. Jake was not close with his father for most of his life. If you wonder why, it's because his father was extremely abusive to him. Ironic, isn't it? Years later, Jake tried to have a relationship with him and his third wife, whom Jake liked. She was a saint.

Jake had a nice truck, a Toyota Tacoma with an access cab with seats for the kids. It was comfortable enough for our 23-hour drive to Florida from NY. Jake would not allow the radio to be on for the entire trip. He said, "We can just talk, we don't need to listen to music." It was a long trip. Once we reached Florida, Jake then wanted to listen to a CD by Willie Nelson. He played one song called "Okeechobee" at least ten times. Jake had lived in Okeechobee, Florida, many years ago so I guess it brought back good memories. The kids and I were glad to have any music on, not having to have these boring conversations with their father anymore.

We were glad to finally arrive at his father's house. They lived close to Disney World. As we walked in, I could see that Jake's sisters had already arrived from up

North. They were sitting on the couch in the living room, looking our way as we walked in. Our kids haven't met most of them and the few they had met, they hadn't seen for many years. I knew the kids were a little uncomfortable, especially Marie, seeing that she was older, but they didn't make it obvious. We were very relieved to see Jake's father doing much better than we imagined. He was sitting in the living room in his wheelchair, visiting with Everyone. He looked pretty good, considering. I hadn't seen most of his family for many years because Jake had kept us away, for his own personal reasons.

Jake's brother was also there, and it had been quite a while since we had seen him. He was always very nice to Shane, and Shane liked him a lot. At one point, while we were there, Jake was yelling at Shane for who knows what reason, and his brother stood up for Shane and told Jake to stop it. I'm sure Jake didn't appreciate that, but his brother didn't care, and I'm sure he complained to me about it later, but I don't remember. His brother took Shane for a walk outside, and later told me how he and Shane had talked. He had said something about not understanding why Jake was so hard on Shane and he was going to talk to him about it. I thanked him for talking to Shane and being there for him during this visit. It made it less stressful for me.

We only stayed a few days and overall, I remember the visit going well. I was glad that Jake could see his father, and I was glad that Marie and Shane could meet the rest of Jake's siblings. It's a shame they didn't get to know their cousins and other relatives. He always kept us far apart. I don't remember anything at all from the 23-hour drive back home. These gaps in my memory strike me as odd, and even a little scary. Perhaps it was uneventful, or else I've blocked it out.

I do remember another trip, about five months later, driving to my sister's house in upstate New York for our traditional family Christmas Party, which took place a couple of weeks before Christmas. We had been doing this for several years and the kids enjoyed it, and so did I. Any chance to see my family was wonderful. During the trip we were listening to the radio and the song "Family Portrait" by the singer, Pink, came on. I remember Marie saying to us, as she listened, "This is our family song." I just felt horrible hearing her say that, but understood why she thought that. Now, as I'm listening to the words of the song, it makes me cringe inside. It was very upsetting. Jake just laughed and didn't even realize that this was not a good thing, that his daughter was being serious and wanted us to understand that something was wrong with our family. It didn't seem to matter what the kids and I ever said to him, he didn't let it sink in or just didn't care. Jake was clueless.

***

(I wish I could share the lyrics, but it's copyrighted) you can listen to the song on YouTube.

Chapter

6

The Beginning
Of
The End

I didn't know it at the time, but the beginning of the end was near in this horrible relationship. I came home from work one evening and found Marie in the kitchen looking a bit frazzled. It was obvious that something bad had happened between them and their father. Marie proceeded to tell me that Jake had gotten angry at her and Shane because they were late coming home from school without permission. She had decided that they would hang out with friends after school to watch the soccer game. She thought Jake and I were both working late, and we would not know what time they got home. Jake ended up getting home from work earlier than expected and when they weren't home, he drove to the school to look for them (or at least, he says he did.) He was very angry.

I had happened to message Marie that Jake was on his way home. Of course, I thought she was already home. Marie saw my text, got her brother and knew they better get home, leaving school before Jake arrived at the school (not knowing he was on his way there). They arrived home before Jake. Their father came in the door a few minutes after them and started screaming and yelling at them, grabbing Marie's arm in anger. He then started screaming at Shane believing that somehow this was his fault. Marie told him that it was her idea, and that Shane was not to blame. She believed his anger was not so much that he'd been worried, but more that they had dared to disobey the "rules" and not be home like they were supposed to be. They were not allowed to stay after school and had to go right home to do chores and homework. I didn't get home for a few hours after this had happened.

From what Marie told me, Jake's screaming and threatening words to them were even more frightening than ever before, and they were really scared, especially Shane. She told me that Shane was up in his room still upset by what happened hours before. I proceeded to go upstairs to check on Shane. Jake was in the bedroom relaxing, watching TV. I don't recall if he said anything to me about their fight or if he acted like nothing happened. All I remember is going into Shane's room to check on him. Shane just looked at me and started crying. He seemed so distraught over everything that had happened earlier. Through his tears he said,

"Why does Dad hate me so much? Why is he

so mean to us?"

It was heartbreaking to see him like that. He continued,

"I feel like I need to stand up to him and

ask him why he is doing this to us."

Here is my 12-year-old son, willing to confront his dad, and his own mother doesn't have the guts to do the same. What was wrong with me? And of course, I didn't want Shane to say anything either because I was afraid it wouldn't go well, but I couldn't tell him he wasn't allowed to do it. I said,

"If you want to you certainly can, but

I don't believe you should."

What was I thinking? I should have said something to Jake about it, not let Shane do it. He had to be scared to death to question his dad about his awful behavior. Needless to say, I didn't do anything, but Shane did.

It had been maybe a half hour since we talked, and Jake and I were sitting up in our bed, watching TV, like usual, except I was feeling very nervous inside, afraid of what might happen, hoping that Shane would say nothing and just let it go. Just then, Shane walked into our room looking nervous and I could see his little body shaking, my sweet boy, just standing there. Jake intimidated all of us, and it was frightening. With Shane's voice hesitating, he said,

"I need to say something to you," Jake ignored him.

"What do you want to say, honey?" I replied.

"I need to ask Dad why he is always yelling at

us and why he's always mad at us?"

Jake was just staring at him now, with this evil, angry look on his face. I could feel the tension and could only imagine how scared Shane was, but before I could say anything, Jake screamed at him. Not a care that his son was asking these questions, just that it pissed him off that Shane had the nerve to ask him this.

Jake started yelling louder than I had ever heard him yell before. His face had turned beet red, and you could just see this look of pure seething anger towards Shane. He was out of control, screaming at Shane, getting ready to jump out of bed to grab him. It was such a blur I don't even remember what Jake was saying I just remember jumping out of bed and getting Shane out of there before it could get any worse. Poor Shane was crying his eyes out, and I focused on calming him down. All the while, I was shaking myself over what just happened. Jake's response was shocking. He was always mean, but I never imagined it would get this bad. I thought for sure he was going to beat the hell out of Shane if I didn't get him out of that room quickly enough. I told Shane we would sit down tomorrow and talk about the situation. This could not continue. I thought I had reassured him that this would never happen again, but obviously, he knew he couldn't trust what I was saying, because nothing I said had ever stopped his father before.

The next afternoon I received a call at work from Shane's school telling me I needed to pick him up. Something had happened and they were not letting him go home on the bus. I knew something serious must have happened, and I immediately left work in a panic. When I arrived at their school, they informed me that my son was too afraid to go home. He told them he was frightened of his father and did not want to go home and be alone with him. They said that I would need to make sure Jake was not at the house before they would let Shane go home with me. He needed to feel safe. Otherwise, they would call child protective services. They said I needed to tell Jake that he had to leave the house for good and not return. I could feel myself shaking as they told me this. I was so afraid of Jake's reaction when he found out, but also relieved knowing that I was being forced to get him out of our lives. This time it had to happen, and Jake couldn't blame anyone but himself, even though I knew he'd blame everyone but himself.

The school kept Shane and sent me home to confront Jake. Jake would already be on his way home, so I waited in our bedroom because I was too afraid to see him come through the kitchen door and have to say something right then. I knew it would surprise him to see my car and wonder why I was already home. Just sitting in my room waiting for him to get home was very nerve-wracking. So much was running through my mind. I remember feeling so nervous; sick to my stomach, but at the same time I felt a sense of relief.

I was going to tell him he had to leave. What was he going to do? What was he going to say? It was unnerving. It was such a mixed bag of emotions, scared, relieved, sad, nervous. Jake could not talk himself out of this one, and we were going to be free from this life of living on eggshells with all the fighting and yelling, which was never for a good reason. As he entered the kitchen, I called for him to come upstairs, just saying,
  "Something has happened, I need
    to talk to you."
Assuming Jake would think it had something to do with my job, I knew he would come up to find out what was going on. I wanted him in the bedroom so he could just grab his stuff and leave with no issues. When he came up the stairs, he started asking me,
  "What is it?"
my voice shaking, feeling sick to my stomach, I told him,
  "Shane is still at school with Marie.
    He told the principal he's too afraid of you
    to come home and told me to go home alone
    and inform you that you must leave the
    house for good, or they will call child protective
    services on both of us."
Jake started yelling in anger, but at the same time started grabbing his stuff, knowing that he had really done it this time. He grabbed his duffle bag out of the

closet while ranting and raving about Shane and the nerve of the school. I just kept hoping he would leave with no incident between us. He finished getting his stuff together and left without a fight between us. He knew this wasn't a fight he would win, but I still thought he would take it out on me, anyway. I didn't have any idea where he would go, but then, I didn't really care. He deserved whatever was happening, and I didn't have any sympathy for him.

As I was driving back to the school, I remember being very nervous, hoping the principal would believe that Jake was truly gone, and allow Shane and Marie to come home with me. The rest is a blur; I don't remember going into the school to get them, but I know they believed me and that's all I cared about. Of course, they knew Shane would let them know if Jake were still there. They never called CPS, trusting I would do the right thing if I didn't want to lose my kids. It was about time I did the right thing for those kids. I certainly never had before. Of course, Shane is the one who did something, not me. We were all in a bit of shock when we got home. It was difficult to believe it was over and that we were free from Jake's constant anger. I can remember thanking Shane for speaking up. I told him he alone saved us from further abuse from his father. I could not take any credit for that.

Shane was so relieved that his father had left, just like we all were, but it wasn't a celebration. It was relief mixed with sadness that it had to come to this, and we didn't know how to process it. How terrible that it to my 12-year-old son to save us from this awful life and not his mother, the adult who should have done this a long time ago. I know Shane felt proud of himself for standing up to Jake and also for telling the school, and he should feel proud of that. His own Mother wasn't strong enough to do it after all those years. I was very ashamed of myself. I hoped life would get easier for the kids now, but there were still some issues that the kids would have to deal with from the years with their father. It wasn't like a light switch and now everything would be great.

A few weeks later, when I was in my bedroom just folding laundry, Shane came in and said,

"I need some help."

I looked at him and asked,

"What's the matter, honey?"

"I think I need to go to the hospital," He replied.

It surprised me to hear him say this, but I wasn't totally shocked, because why wouldn't he be struggling after everything he had been through. Shane had been so brainwashed by Jake into thinking he needed to hurt any kid at school who was mean to him. He had started seriously thinking about hurting the student who was bullying him the most. He was fearful because he felt suicidal and homicidal at the same time. He was afraid he could harm someone. I was proud of him for telling me how he was feeling and having the courage to ask for help.

That very night, Marie and I took Shane to the local hospital emergency room. It was difficult, but it was necessary. Once they brought us into a room and the triage nurse wrote the reason down for our visit, Shane changed his mind. He was backtracking and saying he didn't need help. This was now going to be something I was going to need to enforce, and it would not be easy. This is my 12- year-old son who I was now hoping would be put into the hospital for the help he needed. I can remember us all being in this tiny room, and Shane getting very agitated, pacing back and forth. The doctor came into the room and talked to Shane for a while. Although Shane was acting like he didn't mean what he had said to me, he did share some of what he was feeling with the doctor. Would it be enough for the doctor to see that Shane needed help, or would he think Shane was fine because he played down what he was truly feeling, trying to just go home?

A little while later, a nurse brought in some scrubs for Shane to change into. It wasn't until that moment that we knew they were planning to admit him. They wouldn't ask him to change if he were being sent home. Grateful for this help, it was still very hard to see Shane getting so upset. He started pleading with me, "Please Mom, let's just go home. I am fine." It was heartbreaking. By the time they came back in and told us what was happening, Shane was begging me to take him home. He couldn't believe I was going to make him stay here against his will. I believe Shane thought that he could change his mind and leave. It was difficult for all of us. Marie just sat on a chair in the corner of the room, crying the entire time. I don't even think she uttered a word. She just cried for her brother who she loved so very much.

This hospital had a psychiatric floor for adolescents who needed help to work through these types of issues. When it was time to say goodbye, Shane gave me a hug, but it was obvious how upset he was with me. I knew I was doing the best thing for him, but it didn't make it any easier. All I could do was tell him I loved him and that I would visit him every day. We were all crying at this point. It was terrible that he was going to go through this, and I knew from Tara's hospital stay that his immediate reaction was going to be the worst.

The first day I walked into the unit I could see him sitting in a room across from the nurse's station. I asked the nurse on duty if I could see my son, Shane. She went into the room to tell Shane I was here, then returned saying, "He does not want to see you today." It hurt me, but I understood. I still wanted to see him and give him a big hug. The next day I expected it, so it wasn't as surprising when Shane refused again to see me. On the third day, I was relieved to find out that Shane had agreed to see me, although he was still upset with me. It might not have been the most pleasant visit, but I just wanted to see him and let him know that I loved him no matter what. I could see him every day after that. He became less angry, but more frustrated, because he didn't believe this place was helping him at all. I hoped it was helping, even if Shane thought it wasn't. After two weeks, they sent Shane home with the understanding he would need to follow up with a therapist until he was feeling better about everything.

After the school year ended, we moved out of the Worcester house. It worried me that Jake could show up at our house, and what he might do. Graciously, my sister and her husband offered their summer home to us a few towns away. I had the kids finish the last couple of months of the school year, but I was glad to get Shane away from the kids that were causing him so much anguish. Shane and Marie didn't seem to mind starting at a new school; they were both happy to be leaving

Worcester and leaving the terrible memories of that house. I know Marie was going to miss her friends a lot, but we were close enough that she could still spend time with them outside of school. That made it a little easier for her. Life was changing for the better, and that's all that mattered. I knew it was possible that Jake could show up at my sister's place, but not as likely as it would have been if we had stayed at our house. Jake told me to keep that house, but I knew better, so I put it on the market and sold it quickly. I then filed for a legal separation after a long, painful 25 years together.

Marie, Shane and I were happier than we had ever been before. We felt free from the fear of Jake's anger and all the screaming. We were free from walking on eggshells all the time. It was such a different life. You could come home and feel safe being there. It's not like everything was perfect. The new school brought its own set of issues, but we now had a place where you could go home and talk about your day and not be constantly yelled at. Someone was listening to you and making you feel better about your day. It may not have been our home, but it was a sanctuary for us.

✳✳✳

The kids did not see their father for a few years. They would talk to him on the phone from time to time, but that was it. He moved back to Maine after all this happened, and I was glad, because I knew he was far enough away and wasn't just going to show up on our doorstep without warning. He could have stayed in the area trying to have a better relationship with his kids, but it was easier for him to move away and play the victim instead of admitting to his wrongdoings and trying to make amends.

When Shane was around 15 years old, his father called, asking if Shane would go to a family reunion with him in New Hampshire. I was not comfortable with this, but I knew Shane had been wanting to see his father, thinking maybe things would be different now that he was older. Maybe his father would see the young man Shane had become and treat him with respect and appreciation. I believed that Shane would be safe with the other family members around; my only concern was the drive alone together. I decided to let him go, but made sure Shane had a cell phone so he could keep in touch with me during the drive.

The day arrived for Shane to leave, and Jake was in the driveway. I was anxious, hating the thought that Shane was going to be leaving with him. I kept this to myself because Shane was looking forward to it. I prayed they would make it as far as New Hampshire without an altercation. I hoped that Shane was old enough to handle
.

any issues and knew that he would let me know if he needed me. He was such a smart young man; I needed to give him the benefit of the doubt that he would be okay. Thank heaven for the cell phone. If I couldn't keep in contact with him, I don't think I would have allowed him to go. I was hoping that Jake had learned something from all of this and wanted to change.

To my relief, the trip went well for the first two days. However, a couple nights later I received a call from Shane around 1 AM. He was crying, sobbing, I could barely understand him. Shane was saying,
  "Mom, he grabbed me by the throat,
    I thought he was going to kill me. Mom,
    the look in his eyes, I was so afraid."
I could hear the fear in his voice. I told him,
  "Everything will be all right, I'm coming
    to get you right now. Where are you?"
While Shane and Jake were at his family's campgrounds, Shane and Jake were arguing about how terribly Jake treated Shane and his siblings. Jake said he's never been a bad father, and Shane, thinking he was safe from Jake's wrath because Jake's family was all around, called Jake out on the lies and rebutted everything Jake said. Reminding Jake about arguments, beatings, threats; Shane didn't leave anything out. In what seemed like an instant, Jake had jumped up from his seat and lunged

towards Shane, who was sitting on the couch, and picked him up by the throat, yanking him clear off of his feet and throwing him through the screen door. Shane hit his head on the pavement outside, but that didn't stop him from screaming at the top of his lungs for Jake to "stay the fuck away" from him.

Jake's family had witnessed the incident, and Shane's cousin had run over to help him. Jake's brother-in-law heard the commotion and confronted Jake. When he found out Jake had grabbed him by the throat, Jake's brother-in-law threatened Jake, saying "You grabbed your son by his throat? How the fuck would you like it if I did that to you?" Jake's brother-in-law, being bigger than Jake, made sure Jake stayed clear of Shane while Shane's cousin drove him to his home in Boston that night so he could call me from a safe place. Thank God for him.

The next day, his cousin offered to drive Shane halfway to me and I would meet him there. If Jake had it his way, no one else was going to get involved in helping Shane, and for his cousin to take Shane away, Jake was furious. Jake called his nephew the next morning, demanding directions to his house so he could pick up his son. His nephew explained that he would only do that if Shane was okay with it, which Shane was not going to let that happen. There was nothing Jake could do about it. This was such a devastating turn of events. I knew then that Jake would never change, even though it meant he'd destroy any possibility for a positive relationship with his children.

I felt so angry that this happened to Shane and upset with myself that I let him go. What made me believe Jake could ever change or be decent to him? I knew something bad might happen between them, I just didn't realize how bad it was.

On the drive back home, Shane told me what happened. Shane believed Jake was going to kill him at that very moment but threw him out the door instead. He said the look in his father's eyes was pure hatred. It broke Shane to realize how much his father truly hated him. I felt so bad for Shane; he had wanted this so much, a new beginning with his father, but that would never happen. The next day I filed a restraining order in court.

Jake came to court trying to fight it. There we were in the courtroom, Jake sitting across the aisle from us, crying and telling the judge he would do better, playing down what had happened to Shane. When the judge agreed to the restraining order for two years, Jake started pleading with him, "I cannot go two years without seeing my son. Please, you can't do this to me." The judge told the bailiff to give Jake a copy of Shane's medical records which he had also considered in making his decision. He told Jake that the decision against Jake was more than just his last incident. The judge had read all the hospital records. As Jake sat there looking through the records, he acted surprised by what the doctor's notes revealed, as if he didn't know it had been that bad.

This wouldn't be the only nail in the coffin, though. Shane wrote a letter to the judge, explaining exactly what his father had put him through, his entire life. After reading the letter, the judge granted a two-year restraining order. All I cared about was that the judge made the right decision, and now I wouldn't have to worry about Jake coming anywhere near Shane for the next two years.

I felt like this ordeal, all these years of fearing this man and what he could do and what the kids went through, was finally over. The next time my kids might see their father, and that's only if they wanted to, was when they would all be adults. Shane would turn 18 a month after they lifted the restraining order. Then it would be up to him and his siblings if they chose to allow Jake in their lives.

I could now feel at peace.

Epilogue

My kids tell me I'm a great Mom and say very kind things to me. Inside I feel horrible and such a failure because I know the truth. Yes, maybe now, I help them in any way I can, but it will never erase the past and the damage I have done. Sometimes I just want to cringe when they say how great a Mother I am.

Today, I just received a call from my son Shane, as I sit writing this book, reading and remembering some of the worst times for him. He called to tell me about something he was concerned about, and I guess I reassured him, making him feel better about the situation. After we hung up and I started working on this book again, I got a text from Shane saying, "I don't know what I did to deserve such a loving mother. You are the kindest and most accepting person I've ever met. I love you dearly, and no matter what I feel personally about the situation, I'm so happy to know I have a mother who accepts me with all my flaws, without question or judgment. I love you so much, Mom. You truly are an amazing woman."

What more could a mother want to hear from her child? I just cried, feeling like the worst mother ever. Although moved by what Shane wrote to me, and grateful he could feel that way about me, I felt terrible that I was not that kind of mother when he was growing up. I love my children with all my heart, and regret that I didn't stand up for them. It's not that I wouldn't have died for them, because I would have, but I believed that my role was to protect them from Jake by keeping the peace, calming things down, and not angering him to the point where he might run off with them. Jake had threatened to do it so many times, and I truly believed he was capable of it. I thought I was protecting my children. I was wrong.

I need to write this for my kids so that I can move on from the past. I will never forget the past, nor will I ever deny my involvement in what happened in my kids' lives, and I know my children will never forget either. There is no excuse for what my children went through. All the days, months, and years that they had to tolerate it. The guilt I have will never go away, I don't think I will ever forgive myself, but I need to make a last apology because I can't keep beating myself up in my mind like I have been doing for years now. My kids know I am sorry about what happened, but I want them to know that I truly, now, understand how much of this was my fault too. I can't change the past, all I can do is learn from it and hope that my story will stop another parent from thinking they are doing the best they can by staying in an abusive relationship. All it does is show your children how weak you are. If you cannot stand up for yourself or for them, your children will learn from that, and that is not what you want to teach them. It does not make it better, and it will haunt and hurt your children for the rest of their lives. They may say they forgive you, but it will have a significant impact on their adult life whether you or they realize it.

I know, I have seen it.